THE ENCYCLOPEDIA OF
WATERCOLOR
TECHNIQUES
FOR LANDSCAPE

Clouds by LaVere Hutchings

THE ENCYCLOPEDIA OF
WATERCOLOR TECHNIQUES
FOR LANDSCAPE

HAZEL SOAN

RUNNING PRESS

PHILADELPHIA · LONDON

A QUARTO BOOK

Copyright © 1996 by Quarto Inc.
All rights reserved under the Pan-American and International
Copyright Conventions
First published in the United States in 1996 by
Running Press Book Publishers

9 8 7 6 5 4 3 2 1

Digit on the right indicates the number of this printing

Library of Congress Cataloging-in-Publication
Number 96-67140

ISBN 1-56138-617-0

This book was designed by
Quarto Publishing plc
The Old Brewery
6 Blundell Street
London N7 9BH

Senior editor Kate Kirby
Editor Hazel Harrison
Art editors Liz Brown, Antonio Toma
Designer Julie Francis
Picture researcher Jo Carlill
Photographers Paul Forrester, Colin Bowling
Picture manager Giulia Hetherington
Editorial editor Mark Dartford
Art director Moira Clinch

Typeset by Central Southern Typesetters, Eastbourne
Manufactured in Singapore by Bright Arts (Singapore) Pte Ltd
Printed in China by Leefung-Asco Printers Ltd, China

This book may be ordered by mail from the publisher.
Please include $2.50 for postage and handling.
But try your bookstore first!

Running Press Book Publishers
125 South Twenty-second Street
Philadelphia, Pennsylvania 19103-4399

Contents

Reflections of June by J. H. Taylor

Foreword

Once you have tasted the pleasure of painting in watercolor, you will become addicted. Everything about the medium is aesthetically satisfying: the rich variety of mouthwatering colors, the sensuous sable brushes, the soft white textured papers, and even the paint curling from the tip of the brush in the crystal-clear rinsing water.

The special radiance of watercolor comes from the light being reflected back from the white paper through the transparent layers of color. In watercolor, the quick sketch often buzzes with more life than the labored painting and its layers of overworked washes. The pigments are so lovely in themselves, that the less you try to force them into some prearranged idea, the fresher and more vital your paintings will be. Resist the temptation to fiddle with your watercolor while the wash is drying. The effect is to create overworked areas of color and tired paintings. Freshness and vitality are the appeal and attraction of watercolor both for the painter and the viewer.

Of course you must be in control, but remember the old adage "less is more" and you will be well on your way. The "happy accidents" that characterize watercolor are not always easy to encourage, or control, but will occur more readily if you allow your watercolor a measure of freedom. Don't make too many rules for yourself. Buy a decent sable brush and allow your washes to dry without interference—these are rules enough!

Some people will tell you watercolor is a difficult medium because you cannot correct your mistakes. In fact, once the paint is dry, you can actually lift off color, touch in color, scrub out color, and add new media such as gouache, acrylic, pastel, or crayon to restore a disaster area.

Above all, enjoy yourself. After years of painting in watercolor, I am still overwhelmed by the sheer beauty of colors dried on the palette or laid at random on the test paper, marveling at the attractive patterns they make and the unexplored color combinations I missed.

It is the love of watercolor and joy in the pleasure of painting that will ultimately determine the success of your painting.

Hazel Soan

Tools and Materials

Watercolor artists travel light. Whether you are working indoors or out, the basic equipment is neither cumbersome nor heavy.

The most important piece of equipment is your brush; with an inferior one, you will struggle to make watercolors that satisfy. Good brushes are expensive, but it is better to buy one good size 7 sable with which you can paint both broad washes and fine lines than to buy a whole range of cheaper synthetic brushes of differing sizes. A sable brush will allow you to "feel" the beauty of watercolor even as you mix it in the palette, and it will enable you to make the brushstrokes characteristic of the medium.

Water is the next most important piece of "equipment" (and the heaviest). If you want your watercolors to be vibrant and clear, you **must** keep changing your water.

Jars for water
Use one large jar for rinsing brushes, and have two small water jars for diluting colors.

Brushes
From left: The large mop is for dampening paper, laying large wet washes and lifting color. A flat brush comes in many widths. Buy as large a round sable brush as you can afford and try to supplement that with a smaller one as well. Small oxhair brushes will not give you a good brushstroke but are useful for laying masking fluid.

Paper towels
Anything that mops up water will do. Tissues and rags are used not only to wipe your brushes and absorb extra water, but also to lift color from the paper.

Tube paints
For more and stronger color it is easier to use watercolor paint from tubes. Small tubes will last a long time as long as the lids are kept tightly closed, and paint left on the palette is always reusable in the same way as pans.

Pencils
Sketch out compositions with
a graphite or soft lead pencil.

Erasers
Have a clean eraser or putty
rubber handy for removing
unwanted pencil lines or dried
masking fluid.

Pans
For working outdoors
especially, pans provide quickly
accessible color. Some
colors yield up their pigment
with ease; others need to
be coaxed.

Palettes
Paintboxes come with folding
palettes, but you may need to
supplement these if you work
large or with lots of paint.
China palettes are far more
satisfying to use than plastic
ones and are easier to clean.
Neither are expensive.

Watercolor sketch pads
These come in a variety of sizes and with different
weights of paper. The heavier the paper (140lb as
opposed to 90lb), the less the paper will cockle. If you
work wet, use sheets of 300lb watercolor paper
unless you are prepared to stretch the paper
before use.

Additional Materials

In order to practice the techniques explored in this book, you will need some additional materials, none of which are expensive.

Several of the items shown on these pages are worthwhile additions to your basic watercolor kit and have a variety of uses. Few watercolorists are without small sponges, for example. These are ideal for lifting out color for cloud effects and so on; they are an alternative to brushes as a way of laying washes, and if an area of a painting has gone wrong, you can wash it with a sponge and repaint. A hairdryer is indispensable for cutting down drying time when you are working indoors.

Sponges
The pleasant irregular texture of a natural sponge makes it ideal for applying paint to paper and for washing color out. A man-made sponge is useful for dampening paper or for large washes.

Masking fluid
This is a water-resistant latex fluid used for masking out areas of a painting from a wash. It is sold in bottles from art supply stores, and is available in white and yellow.

WINSOR & NEWTON
À QUARELLE
Fluide
artistique de
masquage
À QUARELLE
Maskiergummi,
flüssig
Fluido para enmascarar pintura
WATER COLOUR
Art Masking
Fluid
75 ml ℮ 2.5 US fl.oz

Candles
White household candles are ideal for wax resist methods. Wax crayons can also be used.

Toothbrush
Any old toothbrush with an even head will do for spattering paint.

Salt crystals
These are used for a special texturing technique. They are scattered into wet paint. Choose large crystals of sea salt and crush them to a finer size with the base of a jar.

White paint
The opacity of white gouache or white watercolor allows the artist to make colors opaque and to restore lost highlights.

Stucco
Ceramic stucco is a textured gel. Mix it with paint to give watercolor real body. The paint keeps its translucency but sets as real texture on the paper.

Hairdryer
To speed up the process of drying watercolor, keep a hairdryer handy in your work area. Be careful not to blow color across the paper, unless of course that is your intention.

Blades
Sharp scalpel blades are needed for scratching out and sgraffito.

Brown gummed tape
You will need to stretch lightweight paper if you are working wet. Use brown tape to hold the paper down on the drawing board.

Ink and dip pen
Ink can be applied to a painting with a dip pen or a brush. It must be waterproof if you don't want it to run or smudge once it dries.

Working Methods

Watercolor is a medium you can use anywhere. It is relatively clean, easily portable, and the materials need little space and little organization.

If you are working sketchbook-size, a small "pan" paintbox with a finger ring can even be balanced in the hand that holds the sketchbook, a small jar of water balanced on the palette of the paint box, and your brush at the ready in the other hand. You can paint standing up, at the bus stop, in the airport lounge, anywhere.

If you are working at home or in a studio, make sure you are looking down on the paper you are painting on as much as possible rather than viewing at an angle. Distortion in a painting is often caused by the angle you are painting at. If you work very dry, you could stand the paper on an easel, but usually watercolorists work quite wet, so you will need to tilt your drawing board as much as possible, without soliciting runs, or sit on a high seat, or even stand over your work. At frequent intervals, step back from your work to view it from a distance. There is nothing more soul-destroying than finding that the painting you thought looked great close up really does not work at a distance. If you find it hard to "see" your own work, look at it in reverse in a mirror. Errors of scale aand perspective quickly show up, and you will find it easier to judge the composition and color balance.

Working outdoors When working outdoors, you will find a small fold-up seat is handy so that you can perch anywhere to make your painting. In addition to your watercolor pad, take a small sketchbook for color notes and sketches. Carry a plentiful supply of water. If you are not comfortable working on your lap, invest in a lightweight easel.

Paper towels on surface to soak up spills and to blot excess water from brushes. If you use white ones, you can also test your colors on them.

Paper is tilted toward the artist to give a head-on view.

The advantage of using a heavy 300-pound paper is that it has no need to be stretched.

Make sure your light source is coming from in front or above, or from the side opposite to your brush; otherwise, you will work in your own shadow.

Four water jars: two for diluting colors (constantly changed), one jar for dirty water, one reservoir of clean water. (This saves repeated trips to the sink).

You can use a mixture of pans and tubes. Often it is a good idea to buy tubes of paint you use often and rely on pans for intense colors you use sparingly.

Plenty of mixing palettes so you can keep reservoirs of clean color.

Never leave brushes head down in water jars. The hairs will bend and splay, and may be impossible to straighten.

Stretching paper

Thin papers will need to be stretched to avoid buckling when wet paint is applied. The ideal method is to dampen the paper and then attach it firmly to the drawing board with brown sticky tape around the edges. As it dries, the paper shrinks evenly because it is held in place by the gummed paper. Check that no edges lift while drying, or buckling will still occur. You then work on the paper while it is attached to the board, only cutting it free when you have finished.

A quick—but not always reliable—method is to tape dry paper down in the same way with either gummed paper or masking tape. As long as you do not get water close to the edges or running under the tape, this method can be a great timesaver. You must always check that the tape is firmly stuck down all around all the time you are painting.

Planning compositions

Composition is the single most important aspect of painting. It can make or break your picture, so it is worth spending time getting it right. If you are out in the landscape, use a small cut-out rectangle in the shape of your paper to help you recreate the landscape on the paper. Mark loosely the half and quarter marks on the side of the viewfinder to help you decide where various elements of the composition will be placed on the page.

Failing a viewfinder, make a rectangle out of the thumbs and index fingers of both hands and look through that.

Use your thumb, a pencil, or the end of the paintbrush held at the end of an outstretched arm to determine relative scale and size between objects in the landscape.

Using photographs

Since the invention of photography, a lot of artists use photographs as a source for their paintings. There is nothing wrong with this; on the contrary, it is an exceedingly useful way of recording shapes and compositions from the landscape. However, if you rely as a beginner on photographs as the source of your paintings, you will not learn to translate three dimensions into two.

It is vital that you sit in front of the subject and select the elements of the painting yourself. If you do not have time for a full-blown painting, make a color sketch.

Colors

There is a vast choice of colors available to the watercolor artist, but you don't need to invest in all or even half of them to make a start.

Many of the colors produced by paint manufacturers go by exotic names the beginner may never have heard of, and which seem to have no relationship with the colors you see around you. But once you have begun to paint and have practiced color mixing, you will begin to think in terms of paint colors, describing something to yourself as yellow ocher rather than brownish/yellowish/gold, or as alizarin crimson rather than dark pinkish red.

As colors are mixed and diluted, you will discover something else, which is that some colors are less transparent than others. Alizarin crimson, for example, is transparent, while cadmium red is semi-opaque. Yellow ocher and raw sienna are similar in color, but the latter is transparent and the former considerably less so.

Begin by choosing a basic range of about 14 colors and get to know them well; you will find you acquire favorites. You may want to add more colors later, but still try to limit the number you use in any one painting.

Earth colors

For entirely naturalistic landscapes, you might try a limited palette of the earth colors. By selecting a few colors, you will more easily maintain a harmony of color throughout the painting.

Terre verte	Aureolin	Yellow ocher
Sepia	Burnt umber	Burnt sienna
Raw sienna	Indian red	Indigo

Beginner's palette

Alternatives are given in some cases, either because two colors are similar enough to do the same job, or because individual manufacturers' pigments differ.

Cadmium red/Winsor red
Alizarin crimson
Lemon yellow/cadmium yellow pale
Cadmium yellow/chrome yellow
Yellow ocher/raw sienna
Burnt sienna

Limited palettes

It is possible to paint with just one color diluted to many tones, and the use of two colors—sometimes mixed, sometimes glazed over each other, and sometimes used alone—presents possibilities for exciting effects as well. Experiment with ultramarine blue and burnt sienna, for example.

With any combination of the three primary colors (red, blue, and yellow), you can, of course, make myriad color combinations. This uses only three colors—alizarin crimson, yellow ocher, and ultramarine blue.

Alizarin crimson   Yellow ochre   Ultramarine blue

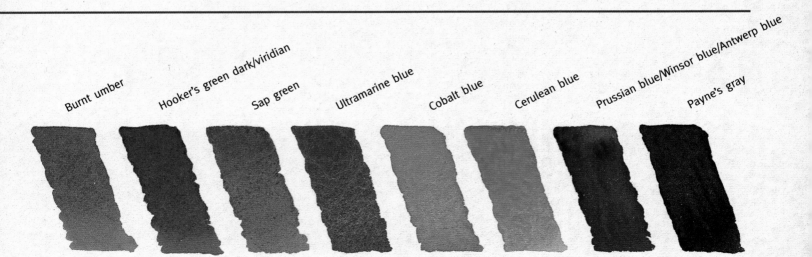

Burnt umber   Hooker's green dark/viridian   Sap green   Ultramarine blue   Cobalt blue   Cerulean blue   Prussian blue/Winsor blue/Antwerp blue   Payne's gray

Landscape greens

Green can be a problematic color in landscape painting. There is a tendency to paint greens too vividly in a childlike manner. To prevent this, why not mix your greens from different blues and yellows, ochers, or siennas? Not only will you find yourself looking more carefully at the green to see whether it veers to yellow or to blue, but you will also find the subtle variations within the mixed color more interesting than laying a ready-made green. Try some of these color combinations for grass greens, tree greens, shadows, and so on.

Cerulean and lemon yellow

Ultramarine and yellow ocher

Prussian blue and aureolin

Raw umber and cobalt blue

Cadmium yellow and cobalt blue

Prussian blue and burnt sienna

Indigo and cadmium yellow

Payne's gray and cadmium yellow

Burnt umber and cerulean blue

Sky blues

The sky forms a large part of many landscape paintings and is often the first area to be painted. There are many different skies shown in the techniques section of the book. The main thing is to make sure the sky harmonizes with the land, so it is often good to incorporate the color you have used for the sky in the landscape itself. For example, the blue of a sky could be used to make the greens of the landscape. Below are some useful hints for choosing suitable blues for different skies.

Warm sky: ultramarine blue

Cool sky: Prussian blue

Mediterranean sky: cobalt blue and cerulean blues mixed

Night sky: indigo, Payne's gray

Warm and cool colors

Colors fall into two distinct categories, described as color "temperature." Some are "warm" and others "cool." Once you start painting landscapes, you will see how important it is to assess the warmth or coolness of the colors you choose. In the Themes section of the book, you will see that artists choose generally cool colors to paint winter landscapes and warmer ones for summer and tropical subjects. Red is warm, and blue is cool. But some reds veer to blue and are therefore cooler reds, and some blues veer to red and are therefore warmer blues. Once you understand this, you can pick a warm blue for a Mediterranean sky or select a cool blue for a winter scene.

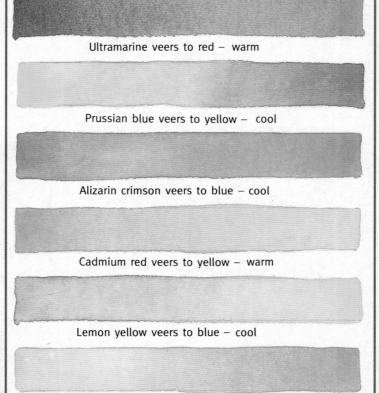

Ultramarine veers to red – warm

Prussian blue veers to yellow – cool

Alizarin crimson veers to blue – cool

Cadmium red veers to yellow – warm

Lemon yellow veers to blue – cool

Cadmium yellow veers to red – warm

Clouds

The grays of clouds are seldom neutral; they are also warm or cool. They may veer to mauve, blue, pink, yellow, etc. Interesting grays can be mixed from two opposite, or complementary, colors. Try ultramarine and burnt sienna; alizarin mixed with viridian; or yellow ocher and cobalt violet.

Ultramarine and burnt umber

Alizarin crimson and viridian

Yellow ocher and cobalt violet

Basic Techniques

Those who have not used watercolor before may find it useful to study the following pages before turning to the landscape techniques section.

Here, you are introduced to the basic watercolor techniques, such as mixing paint, laying washes, working into wet paint, and building up colors by glazing. At the end of the section, methods such as dry brushing, sponging, and masking are introduced as an appetizer for the main techniques section that follows.

You may think it more useful and more pleasurable to practice these techniques in a painting rather than as exercises in themselves, but the beauty of watercolor is that even experimental daubs often make mouthwatering images, and playing with paints and brushes will increase your confidence, too. Simply mixing color in a cool china palette with a soft brush is a pleasure for the watercolor artist.

The medium Watercolor's greatest asset is its transparency, so learn to exploit this to the full. Instead of premixing colors, try the effect of overlaid washes to build up to the color you want. Lay your color crisply, and avoid brushing over and over the same wash; otherwise, the underwash will lift and you will have sacrificed the translucency.

Or try mixing colors on the paper by working wet-in-wet, so that they flow gently into one another. The effect of this is often more exciting than that of premixed colors. But always wait for the paint to dry before judging the results. Watercolor left to dry untouched is almost always lovelier than when tampered with, so don't fiddle with wet-in-wet work or with washes. Mistakes can often be rectified when the paint is dry, with colors lifted or moved around, and edges softened.

Diluting color in the palette

1 Squeeze a small amount of pigment into the palette. Dip your brush into clean water and add to the pigment, blending a small amount to one side, or if you need a lot of paint, blend the whole amount into an even solution. Check there is no unmixed pigment left in the brush before you make your stroke. If you are using pans of paint rather than tubes, rub the clean, wet brush onto the pan of color to release the pigment into the brush.

Diluting color on the paper

Colors can be selectively diluted on the paper itself. This is a useful method when you want variations in tone, for a sky, for example.

1 Paint a small wet wash of strong color onto the paper. Rinse the brush and add pure water to the edge of the color, drawing the strong color out as a wet diluted wash.

2 Lay a small blue wash. Before it dries, use a clean, slightly damp brush to draw the color out in veils from the main pool of color.

Mixing color on the palette

An important thing to remember when mixing colors is that they look much darker on the palette than when applied to paper and left to dry. Try out mixtures on a sheet of sketching paper.

1 | Having already diluted the colors on the palette, blend two together to make a third color.

2 | Ultramarine blue and alizarin crimson mixed together make purple.

3 | Alizarin crimson and yellow ocher mixed to make orange.

4 | Yellow ocher and ultramarine mixed to make a green.

Mixing color on the paper

When one wet color is laid over another, still damp one, the two blend together gently, creating a partial mix that is often more exciting than a flat application of premixed color.

1 | Paint a swatch of the palette-mixed purple in the middle. Then lay down the red and blue separately on either side and drop the other color of the pair into it while it is still wet.

2 | Now try the red and yellow mixture in the same way. Allow the paint to spread into the other color by itself rather than trying to mix it with your brush.

3 | The mixture differs according to which color is laid first. The green produced by dropping blue into ocher (left) is not the same as this one, where ocher is added to blue. Both are different from the palette-mixed color in the center.

Wet-in-wet technique

If you tried the mixing on paper method on the previous page, you will have already taken your first steps in the wet-in-wet technique. Beautiful effects occur as one color spreads into another. You will see the technique used abundantly throughout this book.

3 | Paint a wash of color. While wet, bring another color up against the edge and allow the color to spread untouched into the first color.

Dropping in color

When a wash is wet, more color can be dropped lightly in without disturbing it. The brush is filled with paint, but only the tip is touched to the paper, allowing the new color to run down and into the first wash.

1 | The clean paper is dampened at the top with clear water, and the paint laid just below is allowed to run into the damp paper.

4 | Blending the colors wet-in-wet may look messy when wet, but do not be tempted to play with the wash.

1 | Sap green is dropped into a wet wash of new gamboge by letting the paint run into the color from the tip of the brush.

2 | The color will spread out and if allowed to dry untouched will blend softly.

2 | If the damp paper is nearly dry, only a slight spreading will occur, creating crinkly edges – ideal for distant treelines.

5 | Leave it to dry, and it will create lovely, if unexpected, effects.

3 | Dropping clear water into a wet wash will lighten the tone and create a dappled effect.

4 | Dropping opaque white paint into a wet wash has a more dramatic effect.

Surfaces

Paint dries differently on different surfaces. On smooth (hot-pressed) paper, the paint sits on the surface in pools of color and often dries creating blooms and ragged edges rather than blending smoothly. Interesting effects can be made in this way.

1 A blue wash is applied to hot-pressed paper, leaving white areas for red flowers to be dropped in wet-in-wet.

2 The colors have blended unevenly, pushing the color into blooms and backruns. On standard watercolor paper (cold-pressed, which is rougher), they would be less obvious.

Laying a flat wash

Beginners are often encouraged to practice laying perfectly flat washes, but while it does teach you control of the watercolor, it is a technique that is rarely used to create paintings, except as an underwash for a whole picture.

1 Load the brush and lay the paint in even strokes across the paper from one side to the other. Tilting the board a little will help the bands of color run into each other.

2 Never go back over the wet paint; it will usually dry flat, though it may look uneven while still wet. You can dampen the paper before laying the wash, which helps the colors blend together so that they dry more evenly.

Laying a graduated wash

This is a one-color wash that changes tone as it progresses. Again, mix plenty of color on the palette, but this time, as you lay each successive band of color, gradually add more water to the mixture.

1 **First dry and then wet paper**
Start with a strong solution of yellow ocher and lighten it gradually by the addition of water to each new stroke across the paper. The last band should be almost pure water. If the wash appears slightly uneven, tilt the paper to encourage the paint to flow. Do not touch it with your brush.

2 **On wet paper**
Sometimes a more dramatic tonal gradation is required. Dampen the paper and lay two or three bands of full-strength color, followed by really pale color, and finally pure water for the last stroke. Again tilt the paper to encourage the flow of the paint.

Variegated washes

These are washes blending two or more colors together. A sunset might require linear bands of red, yellow, and blue, whereas a tumultuous sky could be depicted with blobs or splotches of different colors blended in a more irregular way.

1 | Mix your colors before you start. Lay the colors on dry paper in even bands, allowing the wet edges to blend with each other. Resist the temptation to touch up with your brush while the wash is drying.

2 | Dampen the paper then brush in the palest colors. Tilt the paper and allow the colors to blend.

Glazing

Watercolor is a transparent medium, so an overlay of new color allows the one underneath to shine through, creating new colors and tones. This is the very essence of watercolor painting and allows the artist to use few actual colors to achieve many colors on the surface of the painting. Tones can be darkened by glazing.

1 | **Glazing with only one color:**
To glaze with one color, lay a small wash and allow it to dry. Overpaint with a few brushstrokes of the same color.

2 | When it is dry, paint more strokes of the same color over the top. This could be used for a grassy foreground.

3 | **Glazing with different colors:**
Paint a few brushmarks with yellow ocher. When they are dry, overlay with small brushmarks of sap green.

4 | As the paint is drying, touch in brushmarks of darker green. Already you can see how foliage might be built up in this way.

5 | Glazes can be built up in layers to achieve a richness of color. Lay a brushstroke of burnt sienna over a dried patch of yellow ocher. Each successive color leaves some of the undercolor untouched.

Glazing for shadows

Glazing is useful for describing the shaded sides of objects, or for painting cast shadows. It allows you to paint the whole object without having to worry about form until later, or to paint the landscape without having to worry about the shadows until the painting is dry. The undercolor will show through to unify the whole.

1 | Wash in the sky, leave it to dry, and then paint the silhouette of the tree over it.

2 | When the green is dry, delineate the shaded areas with a darker color. For more subtle shading, you could use the same color as the tree for your glaze.

Dry brush

If the pigment is used fairly dry, a broken textural effect is created by the paint dragging over the grain (tooth) of the paper. Before applying the brush to the paper, tap or blot excess moisture from the end of the brush so that the bristles carry pigment but little water between them.

Mix your colors on the palette and prepare your brushstroke as described above. The individual hairs of the brush lay fine parallel lines which can be used for blades of grass, wood grain, and other fine details.

Sponging

A small natural sponge makes an interesting texture of fine marks and dots which would be difficult and laborious to achieve with a brush. The method is particularly suitable for sparse foliage.

The sponge will absorb a lot of the color, so mix plenty of creamy paint in a deep palette. Dip the sponge in the paint and pat the color onto the paper, turning the sponge every time so that the pattern created is not repetitive.

Masking fluid

This rubbery substance is a useful resist for reserving small areas of white paper or lighter color from an overall wash. It dries quickly and can ruin good brushes, so use an old one and wash it immediately in soapy water.

1 Apply the fluid direct from the bottle. For a painting, you should make a preliminary drawing as a guide.

2 When the fluid is dry, paint a wash freely over the masked area.

3 Allow this wash to dry completely, especially the paint that is sitting on the masked areas, then rub the masking fluid off with your finger or a kneaded eraser.

4 Additional glazes can be painted over the reserved highlights. Avoid leaving masking fluid on the paper overnight or drying it with a hairdryer. You may find it lifts the surface of the paper when you remove it.

Techniques

Landscape painting covers a very wide variety of subjects, a selection of which are covered in the following pages. The section is divided alphabetically to make access to the various subjects as easy as possible. Within each section several techniques are suggested as ways to approach a similar theme. The idea is that you might take this book with you into the landscape. On finding yourself overwhelmed before the splendor of a waterfall you wonder where to begin. So why not turn to the Waterfalls section, and perhaps include Rivers and Rocks as well? You may not have thought, for example, of using masking fluid or wax resist to reserve the whites of fast-moving water. If you then need help with the sky look up Skies and Clouds. Even if you find yourself thinking you would not have done it in the way described, at least it will goad you into a confident painting mood. There is no one right way to paint anything; the techniques shown are suggestions, and show how one or several artists might tackle a similar subject matter.

Autumn

The riot of color—with orange, yellow, and red instead of summer green—is the chief appeal of a fall landscape.

Sponging/flicking Experiment with a sponge to paint the speckled effect of distant trees with partially shed leaves, or to create interesting textures on areas of foliage in the foreground and middle distance; and to suggest a scattering of fallen leaves, flick colors across the paper with a loaded brush. Protect the rest of your painting with clean paper, as flicked paint can travel a long way.

Masking To capture the effect of light-colored leaves, reserve the shapes with masking fluid. Use little upturned brushstrokes, smaller in the background to give a perspective effect. Leave some leaves to the imagination. To add foreground interest, mask out some larger leaves and highlight the carpet of leaves on the ground with sharp dabs of masking fluid. When you remove the masking, paint over the resulting white areas with clean transparent washes, varying the colors.

Glazing Build up your foliage with separate dabs of warm colors, letting each under-color shine through and leaving plenty of light. If the painting begins to look over-vivid, calm it down with either a light overall wash or a dabbed wash of blue or mauve.

To create depth contrast the paler foliage with the dark trunks, boughs, and branches. Use a fully loaded brush for the dark tones, letting it unload naturally as you paint to give a variety of different tones.

Further Information
☞
Basic techniques, page 20.

Sponging

Dip a natural sponge into a creamy solution of pigment and press or dab the color onto the paper to create an irregular mottled texture. Working wet-in-wet or wet-in-dry paint will produce different effects.

1 Paint the sky with a pale wash down to just below the tree line. Dip your sponge into a rich mixture of cadmium yellow and press on the paper to describe tree shapes before the wash dries.

2 Build up the tree forms with cadmium orange and sap green, sometimes dabbing the sponge on the wet paint, sometimes on dry. Mix a darker tone to create the shadows of the trees.

3 Wash in the grass and sponge some texture into the foreground. Add a few grass blades with a flick of the brush.

Masking

Protecting light details with masking fluid enables you to paint the composition freely and yet reserve the white paper underneath. Then you can rub off the masking fluid and touch in the details with light transparent glazes or leave white paper.

1 To reserve the lights between the leaves of a loose autumn scene, mask out the highlights before you lay wet-in-wet brushstrokes with a flat brush.

1 Before any color is laid, paint the fluttering leaves with dabs of masking fluid. When all the background washes have been put on, rub off the masking with your finger.

2 Glaze the unmasked leaves with transparent color. It will not matter if you overlap the dark background as you touch them in.

2 Add more masking fluid across the tree-trunks to preserve the light orange leaves before you paint the dark trunks. Rub off the masking and touch in dark orange splashes of color.

3 Paint small glazes over the leaves on the grass using new gamboge, yellow ocher, burnt sienna, and oxide of chromium (green).

Beaches

Beach landscapes conjure up many things—

vacations, chosen loneliness, freedom, romance, and

the elements. Decide what you wish to convey in

your painting before picking up your brush.

Choose warm, bright colors for a vacation atmosphere or seek the earth colors for wild isolation. Before you begin assess the overall colors.

Color and composition Sand, for example, is unlikely to be yellow; it may be a diluted yellow ocher or raw sienna, slightly pinkish, gray, or nearly white. Wet sand is usually darker than dry sand and creates intriguing reflections which you can use to enhance the wetness.

Composition is important. Find a foreground feature to help throw the background into the distance. Sand dunes, rocks, or driftwood give you an opportunity to use some stronger color and tone in the foreground, which will help paler colors in the distance recede (see ROCKS).

Graduated washes The horizontal format of sea and sand, with sky above, lend themselves well to graduated washes. Only dampen the paper down to the crests of waves— or work on dry paper—and do not touch the wash while it is drying. Alternatively, try working on rough-textured paper— the speckles of white paper left untouched by the pigment create natural highlights. For soft shadows in undulating sand, work wet-in-wet, brushing in the shadow color while the first wash is still damp.

Texture Sand textures can be conveyed by flicking and spattering, even by using real textures, such as sugar scattered into a wash or sand mixed with gum arabic.

Further Information
☞
Rocks, page 94.

Flicking

The grainy nature of sand dunes is enhanced by filling a brush with plenty of strong pigment and literally flicking it across the paper in a chosen direction by holding the brush toward the end of the handle.

1 First lay a wash for the sky and sand dunes, dropping darker color into the wet dunes to create undulations in the sand.

2 Protect the sky with a mask of paper, torn to correspond with the line of the dunes. Load the brush with a strong solution of paint and flick the brush diagonally across the paper.

3 After flicking several different colors, remove the paper mask and touch in the grasses with quick upward brushstrokes.

4 | Thicken the grasses with stronger color and cast a warm mauve shadow down the face of the dune. Paint this with single strokes of a wide, flat brush without disturbing the flicked texture.

Graduated washes

A delicate under-painting of graduated washes is a good base for quickly creating the subtle variations of wet and dry sand bordering the sea. Prepare plenty of well-diluted paint before you begin. A few subsequent washes and small details complete the picture.

1 | Separate the sky wash from the beach by leaving dry white paper between them. Use a flat make-up sponge to lay gently graduating washes, increasing the density of color over the sea and below the area of wet sand.

2 | Darken the sea with cerulean and Payne's gray. Just before the beach wash dries, brush in a diluted wash of Payne's gray along the wet sand, letting it spread slightly.

3 | Brush in the rock forms while the wash is still wet and allow the color to run into the wet sand. Darken the rocks with burnt umber.

4 | When the paint is dry, pick out the shadows under the wavelets with fine broken brushstrokes running along the line of reserved white paper.

5 | Paint a few more brushstrokes along the wave lines in the sea and some dry brushmarks across the wet sand and beneath the rocks to emphasize the reflections in wet sand.

Texture

Adding real textures to watercolor paintings creates a pleasant three-dimensional quality to the surface. In this example a palette knife is used to lay a textured gel mixed with paint squeezed direct from the tube.

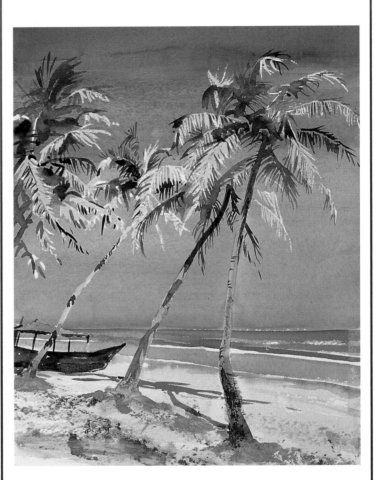

1 The trees are masked out with masking fluid and the sky and sea painted with strong vibrant washes. Paint the beach with a pale wash darkened wet in wet under the wave edge.

2 The palm fronds have been painted. Mix the acrylic texture gel (ceramic stucco) and undiluted burnt sienna with a small palette knife, and scrape the paste across the beach foreground.

3 More textured paste is mixed with sap green and laid over the washes around the trunks of the palms. When dry, a heavier impasto is scraped across the textured areas—leaving satisfying lumps of paint in its wake.

4 The gravely nature of the foreground creates a strong sense of perspective. Paint the shadow of the palm tree across the sand to emphasize the flat white beach beyond the trees.

Bridges

As man-made features in a landscape, bridges bring a change of color and form, making an interesting focal point for a composition.

When bridges are reflected in still or slow-moving water, they seem almost to have been designed for the artist. Before you start, think about the best angle from which to paint. A slightly oblique view showing the shadowy underside of one end of the bridge is more visually interesting than a head-on view. Begin with a pencil drawing, paying special attention to the arc of the underside of the bridge, and give yourself a pencil guide for the reflection also.

Wet-in-wet If the reflection is soft and broken up by moving water, dampen the paper, then blot the ellipse of light and the areas below the reflection with a tissue. When you wash in the paint, it will spread softly to the edges of the damp area. Have a tissue ready to blot any paint that tries to escape over the edges onto the light ellipse.

Paper masking If the bridge is mirrored in still water, the reflection will be crisp and hard-edged. One way to make sure you get a perfect reflected shape in a head-on view is to cut the semi-circular arch out of a doubled piece of paper, and either draw around or paint over it. Look for the shadow cast on the water under the bridge, as this will help to establish the water level. If it confuses the reflection, however, leave it out.

Pen and ink If the bridge itself has become rather "soft," firm it up with fine brush lines or with a little pen and ink drawing. Use touches of pen and ink in other parts of the picture so that the bridge is not isolated.

Wet-in-wet

Dropping paint into a wash before it has dried requires timing. In this case, the area is small and a tissue is used to mop up wayward color. Be bold with your dark mixtures as they may dry lighter than you expect.

1 Masking fluid has been used to reserve highlights. When dry, dampen the paper and lay an overall wash of new gamboge, immediately blotting out the ellipse of light under the bridge with a tissue.

2 While still damp, wash in Winsor green and Prussian blue mixed with new gamboge, and allow the color to spread wet-in-wet. Leave crisp white highlights in the dried area under the bridge.

3 Dampen the river, blot the ellipse, and paint in the reflection of the underside of the bridge, drawing around the bank grasses with the tip of the brush. Drop a darker tone into the wet paint under the bank. Remove the mask, and glaze the leaves and grasses with dabs of light color. Paint the structure of the bridge, leaving the white highlights.

Paper masking

Accurate reflected arches are not easy to draw freehand. Cut a semi-circle out of a folded piece of tracing paper and draw around it to create a reflection that mirrors the bridge arch proportionately.

1 | Sketch the composition in light gray paint with the tip of the brush. Lay the circle of tracing paper in position and sketch lightly around each arch and its reflection.

2 | Wash in sky and foliage equally both above and below the bridge to give a convincing reflection. Strengthen the trees and lay a light glaze over the bridge and its mirror image.

3 | Draw the shadow of the underside of the bridge with the tip of the brush, dropping darker paint into the top of the arch while still wet. Paint the reflection with loose strokes, following your sketch line.

4 | Pick out brickwork details with the tip of the brush, but mirror them in the water with a broad stroke rather than details.

Buildings

Buildings in a landscape tell a story. A small dwelling set beneath hills or mountains may hint at an isolated life, and an ancient ruin can tell of past splendor.

Buildings can also create a focal point, a foreground feature, even just a splash of color or a regular shape contrasting with natural forms. If the building is in the foreground, the texture of its walls will be an important part of the painting. There are various useful tricks for rendering texture in watercolor.

Reserving white paper White buildings such as those adorning Mediterranean landscapes are best reserved as white paper. Define their shapes by using the colors of the landscape around them so that they shine like jewels against the dark terrain, then pick out details with small brushstrokes.

Windows in buildings are like eyes in a face; they add character. Touch them in with wet one-touch strokes of strong varied color, tilting the paper so that more pigment settles either at the top or bottom. This helps to suggest the reflective nature of the glass.

Shadows Follow the same tilting procedure for any shadows under the lintel and to one side of the window to create depth.

Settle your buildings well into the ground. Soften the landward edge with a damp brush, blur it with grasses, or obscure it with foliage. Use the shadow cast by the building to link it to the earth.

Granulated wash Some pigments are "heavier" than others and tend to separate out in a mixture, giving a mottled effect that can be enhanced by working on rough paper. Cerulean, manganese, and ultramarine blues mixed with burnt sienna, alizarin crimson, or yellow ocher make marvelous grainy shadows. The wash must be allowed to dry undisturbed to let the pigment settle.

Wax resist Another way to achieve textures such as stonework or old paintwork is to rub candle wax over the area. The subsequent washes settle only on the unwaxed paper to give a broken-color effect.

Reserving white paper

A light sketch will give you confidence to guide your brush boldly around the shapes of the white buildings. Mix up plenty of pigment and use a size 5, or larger, round brush with a good tip.

1 | Outline the buildings with your brushwork, carrying your wash across the page before it dries around the houses.

2 | Lightly paint the roofs of the distant houses to create a soft mosaic of color. Indicate the windows in the foreground to give confidence to later darker detail. Paint the distant hills with a pale mauve glaze running almost down to the houses.

3 | Finish the foreground details and glaze over the distant houses with the palest of pinks to set them back from the stark whites of the foreground.

Granulated wash

Rough paper, a size 7 brush, and tube color are used to create a granulated wash for the stucco surface of the windmill. Use very wet paint and let the colors mix and settle undisturbed in the tooth of the paper.

1 Ultramarine and burnt sienna have been flooded into dampened paper. When dry, dampen the windmill and its reflection and paint a very wet, loose mixture of cerulean blue, yellow ocher, and burnt sienna. Watch it granulate as it settles.

2 Paint in the banks of the river and use granulating washes on the wall and cottage. Draw the sails with the tip of the brush.

3 When the windmill is dry, paint the windows in with very thick wet paint (indigo and India red); tilt the paper so the paint settles unevenly.

4 Dampen the shaded side of the windmill and, with a strong swift stroke, darken that side against the sky. Lay a broken glaze over the water and paint the foreground details.

Wax resist

Use a white utility candle. Broken white highlights must be drawn with the wax on untouched paper; otherwise, draw the wax over dried washes. Subsequent washes will dry in a mottled patina over the top.

1 Lay a pale ocher and cerulean wash. When dry, draw candle wax over the tops of the parapet walls. Paint a wash of yellow ocher over the waxed areas, and see how it resists the color.

2 The foliage has been painted on dampened paper. Now apply a lot more wax quite heavily over the stonework and rocks, drawing the shapes with the candle.

3 When you lay the next wash of ocher and red-gray, the textured effect becomes much more obvious as blobs of watercolor sit on the waxed surface.

4 Now you can paint stronger color freely over the shadowy rocks while the wax preserves the tonal differences.

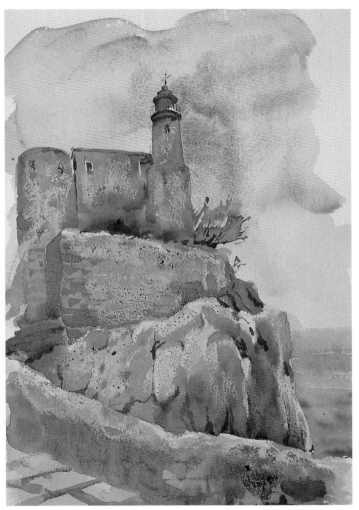

5 Linear brushstrokes, wet-in-wet and wet-on-dry, demarcate the rock shapes and edges of the building.

The blobs left by the dried watercolor create enjoyable textures.

Cliffs

Cliffs can be friendly or forbidding, tall and towering, or low and crumbling, but they are always exciting. They mark the edge of a landscape, a barrier for the sea or plain.

Form and texture are more important than color. But try not to get too complicated; specific cracks and fissures may make it all too fussy and confusing. Look for the outline and the direction of the main forms, and build the face of the cliff with broad tonal washes, using the shadowed areas to create depth. Choose a time when the sun is at an angle to the cliff face, as this makes it easier to discern the three-dimensional forms.

Use the color of the sea or land to emphasize the cliffs, and leave white paper at the base of the cliffs. This can be worked into later to indicate swirling water.

Backruns These are one of the happy accidents that watercolor painters love to exploit. It is impossible to control a backrun completely, but you can give it help. The uneven blooming and feathered edge makes it an effective technique for the surface of rocks and cliffs. Dropping small droplets of water into a wash that has not quite dried can create a mottled texture. When this wash has dried, the structure of the cliffs can be redrawn on top.

Texture methods Grainy sand and scree can be suggested by flicking or spattering paint from a full brush over the surface of the cliffs, and lichen-like effects created by scattering crystals of sea salt onto wet paint (see ROCKS). After the paint has dried, the salt is removed to reveal myriad miniature blooms. Another method is to mix the paint with soap. This destroys its ability to flow, so that it holds the mark of the brush. Linear rock structures can be described with a broad brush, and the small bubbles that develop give the impression of loose stones.

Further Information
☞
Rocks, page 94.

Backruns

This painting uses hard-pressed paper (HP), as it is easier to encourage backruns on a smooth surface where the paint sits in pools. Mix rich dense solutions of pigment to avoid having to darken areas later and lose your initial effects.

1 With a large brush, wash in the sky and cliff shapes, reserving white paper for the surf. Drop deep Prussian blue into the wet shadowy surfaces.

2 Plunge pure cadmium red and alizarin crimson into the bases of the wet shadows and allow the paint to spread and bloom unconditionally.

3 Let the dense pools of color dry untouched, then paint in the strongest darks with almost undiluted indigo.

3 | Mix Prussian blue and scarlet lake for the dark shadows, keeping the suds already in the brush head but without adding more. Pick out the crevices.

4 | Last, delineate crevices and cracks in the formation of the rocks and deepen the shaded sides of the breaking waves.

Soap

Mixing pigment with soap allows you to work into wet paint without the brushstroke spreading. The paint dries with a slight mottling. Use a bar of white soap and rub your wet brush full of pigment into it.

1 | The main forms of the cliff face are painted with Prussian blue. Leave white paper at the base for the surf.

2 | Fill your brush with a rich mixture of yellow ocher and rub the brush into the bar of soap. Paint the strokes in the direction of the rock face.

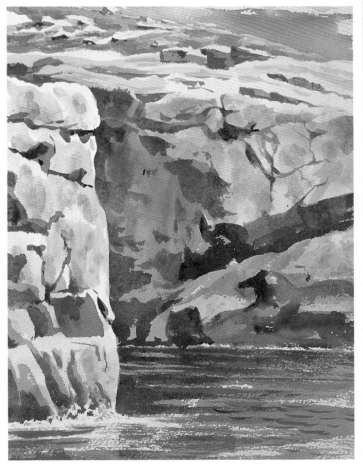

4 | Rinse the brush thoroughly and paint the grass on the cliff top with a wash of blue and ocher. Describe and darken the sea with dark dry brushstrokes.

Clouds

Watercolor lends itself to the ethereal yet solid appearance of clouds. The white paper makes the most of their luminosity, while happy accidents can be exploited to good effect.

Two things to remember are: firstly, to keep your water sparkling clean and, secondly, to avoid overworking your sky.
Wet-in-wet/wet-on-dry A mixture of hard and soft edges is an effective combination for cumulus clouds, which are often crisply defined at the tops and soft and blurred at the bottoms. Dampen the paper in the areas under the clouds and keep it dry above them. Take the blue wash for the sky around the tops to describe the shapes, and drop darker colors into their wet bases to create their bulky forms.

Lifting out Alternatively, try lifting out the clouds with a dry brush, tissue or sponge while the sky wash is still damp. The paint needs to be nearly dry for the best effects or the sky color will just re-run into the areas you have dabbed out. Clouds are always on the move; suggest wind direction by making your clouds full upwind and trailing away downwind.

The dropping-in method is also ideal for heavy storm clouds. Try not to touch the surface with more than just the tip of your heavily loaded brush. Let the color drop gently in and spread out. Tilt the paper to help guide the flow of the paint in the required direction.

For the soft wispy high clouds, dampen the whole area then wash in the sky, leaving larger areas than you require for the clouds to allow the paint to spread over the damp surface.

Wet-in-wet/ wet-on-dry

Work with a large round brush to avoid getting bogged down with detail. Make sure the paper is stretched or heavy enough that you can slosh water around without causing the paper to crinkle.

1 Lay a wash of Prussian blue to outline the main cloud shapes. Dampen the paper above the lower clouds and wash in more color.

2 With a mixture of Prussian blue and alizarin crimson, darken the base of the cloud bank. Run the sea into the bottom of the wash just before it dries to make a soft horizon.

3 Wet the paper from the base of individual cloud masses almost to their tops, drop in more color, and allow it to spread upward to describe each soft shape.

4 Darken the bases of the cloud bank with stronger color, wet-on-dry, and, while it is still wet, drop even more color in from the base.

5 Dampen and darken any clouds you feel need more volume, and finally, hint at the receding cloud bases above the horizon with irregular linear strokes of pale gray.

Lifting out

Using a dry sponge or a tissue to lift out clouds from a wash creates soft, indefinite cloud forms, but never restores the white paper to its full untouched luminosity.

1 Lift white cirrus-style clouds out of a cobalt and ultramarine wash with a piece of tissue before the wash has a chance to dry.

2 Lift streaky clouds out of the same wash with a few cotton swabs dragged across the paper.

3 Alternatively, lay a loose wash of ultramarine and wash in a base tone for the landscape.

4 Mop out the cloud forms with paper towels in bold, swirling movements.

5 Repeat the process of laying washes and mopping out until you are satisfied with the resultant cloud forms.

Dropping in color

Dropping or brushing in solutions of color into wet paper or wet washes allows the paint to spread in the soft, almost controllable, manner so characteristic of watercolor.

1 For a simple fair-weather sky, wet the whole paper, and brush selected areas with a mixture of cobalt and cerulean.

2 Lighten the color toward the horizon and, as it is drying, move the color gently around for the required cloud effect or simply leave untouched.

3 For more dramatic cloud effects, lay large wet washes of color onto dry paper: Naples yellow, cerulean, and cobalt.

4 Wet the heavy clouds and drop in a mixture of Payne's gray, vermilion, and indigo.

5 Tilt the paper to encourage the pigment to concentrate in the base of the black cloud.

6 Drop pure vermilion into the damp base of the large black cloud and prevent it from spreading too far upward by again tilting the paper downward.

7 Drop in more vermilion and lift out the sun's rays with the side of a damp brush.

Deserts

Deserts may seem hot, dusty, dry, and visually uneventful, yet the very simplicity of a single twisted tree in a flat desert landscape can make a dynamic painting.

To create the impression of heat, use warm colors such as India red, burnt sienna, yellow ocher, reds, and oranges. Use stark shadows to model rocks, stones, and tree trunks, and to reinforce the hot feel, try painting the sky in a similar warm color to the landscape.

Graduated wash Horizontal washes of differing earth colors will emphasize a flat landscape. A graduated wash, strong at the top, fading toward the horizon and strengthening once again into the foreground will establish a good base upon which to build detail.

Sponging and spattering For scrubby trees, dip a small natural sponge into a pool of color and dab it once or twice to create interesting foliage effects. Branches and tree trunks can be added before the paint has dried so that the colors run into each other.

The random effects created by spattering or flicking paint from the brush are ideal for sand or gravel. Make the blobs larger in the foreground to help establish distance.

Wet-in-wet Dust and soft early-morning mists are often features of deserts. Work on damp paper so that color spreads gently into white paper with no hard edges. Paint features that emerge through the dust or mist in flat, pale tones; but in the foreground, suggest the terrain with thorny bushes or grass painted with a dry brush, or rocks and plants dark against light.

Further Information
☞
Pathways, page 82.

Graduated wash/ sponging/spatter

Dampen the paper all over before laying your wash. Apply the wash in horizontal strokes with a large brush. To spatter paint, hold the toothbrush face up above the paper and run your finger backward across the top of the loaded brush.

1 Make the horizon area the lightest part of your graduated wash, refilling the brush for the foreground. Brush horizontal streaks of light red into the wash while it is wet.

2 Use the vehicle tracks to emphasize perspective. Paint the distant hills across the lightest area of the dried wash and use the same color for the tree.

3 Mix up a dense solution of greenish pigment. Dip a natural sponge into the paint and then dab the corner of the sponge onto the paper to create scrubby trees.

2 When dry, paint the trees emerging from the mist; paint the base of their trunks with clear water, and coax the color gently into the water so that the color disappears.

3 Create tufts of grass by dropping color into the base of dampened patches. Using dry paint straight from the tube, splay the hairs of the brush and paint the foreground grasses.

4 Detail the tree root and finally spatter the foreground with a paint-filled toothbrush, or flick color from the end of a brush (see PATHWAYS).

Wet-in-wet

You will only need to dampen the paper in the area of the mist, enough to allow the color to spread gently, but not so much as to cause pools. Watch the mist as it dries to make sure that no hard edges develop.

1 Lay a sky and foreground wash onto damp paper, let it dry, and then wet the area in the middle again. Paint the peaks of the dunes and allow the color to spread down, then turn the board upside-down to prevent further spread.

4 Create small white rocks by reserving white paper in the original wash; give these dark under-shadows, and add the foreground tree to throw back the distance.

Distance

Like layers of fine tissue, overlapping hills gently dissolve into the sky. In a seascape, the water retreats to the palest of hues and merges with the distant horizon.

These lovely effects are caused by our planet's moisture-laden atmosphere—if you were painting on the moon, you could only show distance by means of perspective.

There are three main ways of creating distance in a painting. The first is the use of tonal contrast, which is usually much stronger in the foreground. The second is the use of color. Colors such as blue, blue-gray, and blue-green recede, whereas the warm reds, yellows, and red-browns advance to the front of the picture. The third is perspective—the apparent shrinking of features or narrowing of roads as they move away from the viewer.

Graduated wash For a distant view of the sea, or any flat landscape where the sky and the land become one, a graduated wash is ideal. Keep it dark at the top of the page, lightening toward the horizon. Paint any distant features in flat, unmodeled brushstrokes, keeping them as simple as possible. Lift out any unwanted hard edges or dark tones with a damp brush or sponge.

Glazing If you are painting the receding layers of distant hills, mix mauve or gray-blue to several different strengths. Work from back to front, letting each successive layer reveal a larger area of the previous wash so that the hills grow stronger as they advance. Use darker tones as you come forward, and for the nearest hills, add a little "local" (i.e. the natural) color.

Graduated wash

In this painting, the graduated wash is laid on dry paper to reserve some white for the clouds. Use a broad, flat 1-inch brush and lay a pale wash, lighter at the horizon, darker in the foreground.

1 After laying the pale wash all over the paper, establish the horizon line with a thin horizontal wash and, to soften the sea edge, soak up the color with a tissue.

2 Paint a strong wet wash into the foreground sea and paint the rocks to establish perspective: larger and darker to the fore; smaller, paler, and less distinct in the distance.

3 Add some color to the sky with pale wet washes and touch in the distant hills with the same pale gray-blue.

4 Details in the foreground serve to push the background into the distance —you can almost feel the curvature of the earth!

Glazing

For each glaze, mix plenty of pigment before you lay the paint. Use a large brush and lay subsequent washes gently and with single strokes so you do not disturb the washes underneath. Use the same color, but dilute less each time.

2 Repeat the glaze over dry paint, again leaving the top of the last ridge exposed. Use this wash to describe the foreground slopes.

3 Brush in the foreground; add a darker glaze to indicate the trees in the valley and hint at fields on the middle-distance slopes.

1 Lay an overall underwash to unify the painting. When dry, lay a darker wash over the top to outline the hills. When this dries, repeat the glaze, but leave the farthest peaks peeping out above.

4 Touch in foreground details with local color: browns and greens to emphasize the foreground and to help the distance recede.

Fields

It is hard to pinpoint the fascination of fields.

Perhaps they appeal because they are the man-

made face of landscape.

Or perhaps the attraction is the rich array of shapes and colors
—patchwork patterns retreating up a hillside; parallel strips of
freshly plowed earth; swaying expanses of flower-strewn
golden wheat.

Wet-in-wet Vary your technique also, using touches of wet-in-
wet for soft distant features and for hedges bordering the fields.
In the latter case, dampen the paper above the edge of the field
and run a broken line of color along it. The color will spread
upward into the damp paper in irregular shapes like the growth
of a hedge. Strengthen some areas with more color while the
paint is still damp.

Overlapping washes The pattern of fields in the middle
distance can be built up with overlapping washes of
transparent color—ochers, mauves, greens, yellows, browns.
Don't let them become monotonous—use broken color in
places to suggest texture, and bring in shadows made by
clouds, trees, and hedges to break up solid color.

For furrowed fields, use just three tones—a pale one over
the whole area, a second to delineate the furrows with fairly
thick lines, and finally a dark tone for the thin, deep shadows
along each furrow.

Masking Field paintings often need some foreground interest.
Use masking fluid to pick out some vertical stalks of grain,
either *en masse* at the edge of a pathway, or as individual stalks
against fence posts or at the front of a field. You can
treat a few flowerheads among many in the same way.
Create an immediate sense of perspective by painting
larger ears of wheat—or poppies, for example—in the
foreground, dwindling in size as they recede until they
become a mass of color.

Three tones for the furrowed field

The three tones chosen to
paint the furrows of the field
must be fairly close in color
and varied enough in tone.
The overall underwash is your
lightest tone.

1 **Tone 1** Paint a light
wash of cadmium yellow,
leaving a few scattered areas
of white paper peeping
through.

2 **Tone 2** With a mixture
of cadmium yellow and
burnt sienna, draw lines to
mark the field's furrows. Use
the same color, mixed with
green, for the distant hedges
and foreground tree.

3 **Tone 3** Mix a darker
tone of cadmium yellow
and burnt sienna. Create a
deep shadow by drawing it
along one side of the furrow.
Use the same color for the
hedge.

2 | Mask out a few daisy heads in the foreground. With a size 4 brush, lay diagonal strokes of color between the poppies: yellow ocher, cerulean, green, and lilac.

3 | Continue overlapping diagonal brushmarks until you have built up a lively pattern of color. Describe the petaled heads of the poppies with small, dark red brushmarks.

4 | Tighten up the division between the fields with touches of dark violet, and strengthen the tree and grasses with the same complementary color.

Overlapping washes

Mix a variety of bright translucent colors in the palette or work straight from pans. The variety of colors increases as each overlaps the other in a lively mosaic, suggesting the shimmering movement of grasses.

1 | Lay out your poppies in scarlet lake and vermilion. With short, lively brushstrokes, paint the distant fields and trees in a variety of over-lapping colors.

4 | Work the same colors into the background to marry with the foreground colors, and push shadow under the poppies to bring them out. Rub off the masking for the daisies.

Masking

Paint the masking fluid straight from the jar with an old brush. Alternatively, you can protect a good brush by coating the hairs with petroleum jelly. Remove the masking only when the painting is completely dry.

1 Mask out the foreground grasses, fence posts, and furrows in the middle distance. When dry, paint a yellow wash over the masking and up to the sky wash.

2 While damp, brush siennas and greens into the foreground and delineate the hedges and bushes by dropping color into the damp paint.

3 Bring darker color into the left-hand bush to contrast with the light masked area. When completely dry, rub off the masking fluid with your fingers.

4 Paint in the fence posts and foreground grasses with a fine brush, keeping them light against dark or painting them dark against light.

5 Dampen the fence posts and drop darker color down one side to create a three-dimensional effect. Draw lines along the gatepost to make it stand out against the pale background.

Foliage

There are no rules here – the foliage of trees, shrubs and bushes can be painted in so many ways and with so many techniques.

It is important to establish the foliage masses before engaging with detail. Half close your eyes and look for the shapes of the trees and the main lights and darks. Paint these in with broad washes in a neutral tone such as Payne's gray. If you want a soft finish, paint slightly wet-in-wet.

Brushmarks The most commonly used technique for painting foliage is simply the brushstroke itself. The shape and size of the head of the brush will determine the different leaf shapes, so it is worth a little experimentation beforehand. Dappled foliage against the light is very effectively painted with successive dabs of color. Build them up one upon the other but leave plenty of white paper shining through in between.

Reserving white paper The freshest highlights are created by reserving small areas of white paper. You will need to determine the placing of these before you begin to apply color, so make a light underdrawing.

Masking If you are using masking fluid, paint it on in leaf-like dabs with as pointed a brush as possible. The masking can be removed gradually so that glazes of color are built up in reverse, leaving a little on until the end for pure white highlights.

Sponging A whole mass of foliage can be built up by sponging. The first layer should be fairly light and bright in color, with successive layers going darker and less green. Sap green is an excellent green to use for foliage, mixed with Payne's gray for the darker areas.

Wet in wet/backruns Clumps of foliage can be rendered by dampening the area of the bush and dropping color in at the base. The color spreads upward, leaving the topmost portion of the bush as the lightest.

If you are painting large masses of foliage allow backruns and blooms to develop. The textures they create will enhance the living nature of the foliage.

Brushmarks

The brushmark itself creates the leafy foliage. Use a size 6 round brush with a good point. The body of the brush carries the pigment, and the tip dispenses it as you determine what to paint.

1 Paint the fronds of the rhus tree with quick single brushstrokes from the point of the leaf to the stem. Overlay lighter leaves with darker ones, leaving white paper peeping through.

2 For the areas of shadow, brush in dark splodges of monestial green. Mix in a touch of red to kill the greenness.

3 Continue to lay dark strokes to build up the leaf fronds, and paint dashes of cadmium yellow over shadowy washes. Violet is used for the shadows under the tree.

Masking

To create gesture and rhythm throughout your composition, apply the masking with a ¼-inch hog-bristle brush in the main directions of the foliage masses.

1 Mask the highlights on the ground, leaves, and flowers. When dry, paint a very wet merging wash of viridian and sap green.

2 Mask out more individual leaves, indicating the rhythms of growth. Brush lilac across the dried masking and into the shadowy areas.

3 More masking is laid to preserve the under-color. Wash in the deep shadows of indigo and ultramarine blue.

Wait until it is completely dry before rubbing off the masking with your finger.

4 Glaze over white masked-out areas with pink for the flowers and Naples yellow over the pathway. Often you will find that you add back the very color of the masking fluid itself.

Sponging

The irregular texture of the natural sponge is employed to make broad soft washes instead of using a brush, and to create a broken, speckled texture for the foliage. A tracing paper stencil is used to paint the tree trunks.

1 Load the sponge with rich creamy paint, and dab, stroke, and twist it over a wet brushed-on underwash of various greens, emphasizing the volume of the shrubs.

2 Overlay the brushed shadows of the path with a deep, warm sienna taken into the base of the bushes.

3 Cut two pieces of tracing paper and lay them on the painting with a narrow gap between. Hold down the paper and drag a clean, damp sponge downward to remove the color in a straight line.

4 For the dark tree trunks, dab color with the sponge between the stenciled gap. The regular columns contrast well with the sponged foliage.

Wet-in-wet/backruns

Use a large brush to lay your wet-in-wet washes, allowing the colors to spread freely into each other. It does not matter how uncontrolled the foliage appears at first because you can tighten it up later.

1 Hint at the structure of the rose bower; then with a flat 1-inch brush, lay greens and blues to suggest the areas of light and dark foliage. Let them merge wet-in-wet.

2 Fill a size 5 round brush with alizarin crimson, mixed with white, and press it into the wet washes to create the soft, round forms of the roses.

3 Crisp up the edges of the lighter foliage by wetting the darks nearby. Draw the brush descriptively around the leaves and let the paint spread softly into the wetted area.

Foregrounds

Foreground emphasis helps to create space by pushing distance further away. It also attracts the eye and takes attention from any over-worked areas in the background.

If you are taking photographs of views to paint at home, find a view of the subject that includes a foreground feature. Take two shots; one with the main view in focus, and the other with the foreground in focus. A quick sketch done on the spot will remind you of the relative proportions of the distance to the foreground detail.

From back to front In general you will find it better to work from the background towards the foreground, because otherwise you won't be able to judge the strength of tone and color you need. But because you will need to reserve white paper for highlights and other light areas, it is a good idea to work out your foreground and lightly brush in the main features at the outset.

Fine detail A way to create small linear pure white highlights, such as those on fence wires, blades of grass or narrow branches, is to scratch off dry paint with a scalpel blade. For foreground grasses, or for the textures of wood, the dry-brush method is ideal.

Masking Use masking fluid to retain highlights on small foreground features, and reserve the white paper on larger areas by taking washes around the shapes. Rubbing masking fluid off slightly scuffs the paper surface, so you don't want to use it in areas where the freshness of the watercolor over the white paper is all-important.

Scratching off

A sharp-pointed scalpel blade is ideal for scratching off the painted surface to reveal pristine white paper underneath. The heavier the paper, the more confidently you will be able to scratch. This example uses 250 pound.

1 Lay a pale wash for the sky and background fields, strengthening and varying it as it comes into the foreground. Paint the poppies with strong positive strokes.

2 Paint dark green washes on each side of imagined stems and strands of wheat; this is called painting negative shapes.

3 Scratch out stalks and pods with the point and side of the scalpel, roughen the paper with the blade, and then pull out to expose the pure white paper.

Masking

An old, worn-down size 2 brush is used to apply the masking fluid onto the clean paper. Let it dry completely before applying any paint. Finer features can be masked out with the nib of a dip pen.

3 Remove the masking when the paint is dry and draw individual blades of grass, dark against light, with the tip of the brush.

1 Reserve the tall, swaying grasses with masking fluid painted with an old brush. Wash the background over the top, wet-in-wet.

4 Wet the unmasked white of the flowers and drop scarlet lake into the bottom of each one to create a strong foreground feature.

2 Touch in the hill shadows and field patterns while the wash is wet to create a soft, hazy background. Pick out broad shadows in the foreground rocks.

Forests

The dramatic light thrown between tree trunks by the low sun, or the sheer magnitude of a forest seen from above, presents glorious opportunities for the painter.

Be selective, remember the saying about not seeing the wood for the trees. You are under no obligation to paint every tree, so try to organize your painting to create the essence of the subject. Usually forests are deep in color. Be bold; mix strong solutions with a lot of pigment.

Wax resist To paint a quick rendering of a forest of tall straight trunks, wax resist is an ideal technique. Draw the foreground trunks with the stem of a household candle, then lay a wash, leave it to dry and with each wash draw in the trees behind. Repeat the process, each time drawing more of the trunks, and making them thinner as they recede into the background. Wax resist is also perfect for the texture of individual trunks.

Masking Rubbed and scuffed masking fluid is useful for textures and ragged edges, and you can reserve interesting patterns of light on bark in this way. To mask out whole tree trunks, you can use torn strips of paper, but beware of the paint settling at the edges.

Overlaid washes Building up the forest with layers of transparent washes makes for a rich watercolor with a lot of depth. This technique works well for both a close-up view within the forest and for a panoramic overview. With each wash, some of the previous wash is left showing through, so that with very few pigments you can create myriad colors and tones.

Wax resist

An ordinary white wax candle is rubbed over underwashes to preserve the irregular light cast between the trunks of forest trees. Laying the wax resist allows you to work very freely with bold brushstrokes.

1 Paint a pale lemon and burnt sienna wash over the whole image. Rub wax over the areas where the light is strongest. Paint darker greens in sloshy verticals to loosely describe the trunks.

2 Wax out the light areas again while the wash is still wet, extending the wax over the light colors and tree trunks.

3 | Paint over the waxed areas with a deep sap green and strengthen the tree trunks with Payne's gray and Prussian blue.

4 | Wash burnt sienna over the forest floor and up into the left-hand tree trunks. The wax resist creates a vibrant texture.

Masking with tape

Low-tack masking tape is laid on the paper to reserve the light sides to the trunks and the slivers of light sky peeping through the columns of trees. Hot-pressed paper is used to make crisp edges for the washes.

1 | Place the masking tape over selected parts of the forest and wash over the stuck-down tape with cyanine blue.

2 | Peel off the masking tape carefully and paint green, blue, and gray vertical washes to describe the trunks of trees and the intervals between them.

3 | Re-lay the masking tape, slightly overlapping the original positions and wash color up to and over the edges.

4 | Take off the masking tape and work into the trees, leaving the light sides of the trunks as untouched white paper. Use the tip of the brush to paint the small spiky branches.

Gardens

Their wealth of color makes gardens an ideal small-scale landscape subject, suiting both broad and detailed approaches.

Any of the techniques described in this book can be employed to great effect in a garden scene. There are two potential pitfalls, however. You can easily create confusion by a lack of form or composition; and you can get so carried away with colors that in the end they cancel each other out. The use of complementary colors—those that fall opposite one another on the color wheel—will greatly enhance the brightness of your flowers. Set red flowers in blue-green foliage, yellow against mauve, and orange against blue.

Brushmarks A lively, loose impression can be created using dabbing brushstrokes for the flowers and leaves. Leave touches of white paper in between for the highlights. Pay attention to the tonal (light and dark) structure of the painting; it is easier to assess tone if you look at the subject through half-closed eyes.

Hard and soft edges Try to build the forms of flowering shrubs with light and dark versions of the flower colors. For example, dampen a bush or shrub all over, then drop a strong touch of color into the base and along the shaded side. As the color spreads, it will create a soft, rounded form.

Individual flower shapes can be reserved as hard-edged shapes by leaving dry patches when the paper is dampened in preparation for a wash. The paint will flow around these dry areas, which can be touched in with transparent color when the wash is dry.

Alternatively, the color of the flowers could be painted first and the foliage wash laid on top, reserving the flower shapes as you paint.

Masking Light details are easily reserved with masking fluid. Flowers highlighted against a dark wash can be masked out before the wash is laid. Paint on the fluid in specific shapes rather than indiscriminate blobs.

Wet-in-wet/ wet-on-dry

Use the wet-in-wet washes to create the soft, rounded forms of the topiary and shrubs. Re-wet areas that have dried with clean water. Keep the shadows on the lawn crisply edged to suggest strong sunlight.

1 Paint the main topiary forms in yellow over a pale, drying wash. Drop viridian in patches while wet and let the dark shadow colors spread upward from the base.

2 Lay a pink wash for the flowers and drop deep yellow into that wash while wet. Before the wash dries, paint the shadows of the lawn out from the base of the shrubs.

3 Push darker shadow into the base of the bushes and across the lawn, using the tip of the brush to paint around the flower shapes with crisp edges, but slightly dampen the greenery so that the washes merge.

2 | Build up the background and general foreground quickly, in the knowledge that the flower and leaf details are protected by the frisket.

4 | Paint the deeper shadows on the lawn and trees over the dried washes, and then use clear water to spread the color gently with the brush.

Masking

Masking fluid is painted in specific flower and leaf shapes with a small brush so that a general unifying green wash can be laid over almost all the composition. If you are in a hurry, this will save a lot of time!

1 | Over dried masking, paint a sap-green wash landscape with cerulean dropped into a dampened sky.

3 | Paint the dark shadow across the lawn and darks into the clumps of flowers.

4 | Rub off the masking with a kneaded eraser only when you are sure all the dark washes are in place.

5 | Touch in the exposed areas of white paper with transparent pinks, yellows, mauves, and blues to identify the flowers.

Brushmarks

Use a size 10 round brush with a good tip and a smaller size 4. Let the shapes they make as you first lay down color remain as intact as possible—in other words, let the brushmarks keep their own identity without too much pushing around!

4 Use the size 10 brush and, with lively dabs of color, paint the foliage and flowers. Leave white paper in between for the glimmers of sunlight.

1 Lightly sketch the composition and lay a wet-in-wet wash all around the pots on the patio.

2 Paint a mid-tone background of trees over dry paint, retaining the brushmarks. Use a finer brush to draw in the shadows across the patio.

5 Strengthen the shaded sides of the pots, and boldly darken the unlit sides of the foliage with a mixture of Payne's gray, sap green, and India red.

3 Darken the background trees with Payne's gray. Make the paint quite strong to bring out the sunlight on the potted plants.

Grass

The rich green carpet that covers so much of the landscape looks easy to paint. Yet it presents problems, mainly because the precise color is difficult to ascertain.

The easiest way to decide is by comparison; ask yourself if the grass is more yellow, more blue, darker or lighter, than a tree or other green landscape feature. It pays to take your time, testing the mixture before applying. Trying to correct an incorrect color takes much longer than laying the initial wash.

Rather than paint one uniform wash, vary it slightly to suggest the contour of the ground. When the wash is dry, a few horizontal brushstrokes of the same wash will add interest.

Color There are few grass greens you can use straight from the tube, though sap green is a good strong color, and Hooker's Green Dark is appropriate for shaded grass. Try mixing various blues and yellows, for example cerulean blue mixed with lemon yellow gives a really verdant green for small highlit areas and Prussian blue mixed with different yellows, including yellow ocher, makes a number of very versatile greens.

Sgraffito To describe individual blades of grass in the foreground, try scratching into dry paint with a scalpel blade to reveal the wash or white paper underneath. Don't do this if you want to lay farther washes on top, as it will scuff the paper. A less defined effect can be created by scratching lines out with your thumbnail just before the wash dries.

Masking To reserve light-colored foreground grasses or grasses growing up against walls, rocks or fence posts, mask out individual blades with masking fluid using a fine brush or the nib of a pen.

Dry brush Positive clumps of grass can be painted with a flat dry brush or the splayed hairs of a round brush. Use different colors to create depth and keep the dry pigment quite strong.

Sgraffito

Using the blade of a knife to scratch through the surface color to reveal the one underneath is termed sgraffito. With watercolor it usually means scratching through to reveal the white paper, but with gentle pressure the underwash can be exposed.

1 Paint the field and grasses with successive washes to build up a strong dark body of color. At least one wash can be rubbed in with a tissue to make sure the paper is well stained.

2 While the paper is still slightly damp, scratch out narrow gestural lines not to lift the damp paper, but just to make a pathway through the paint.

3 When dry, be much more forceful with more selective knife strokes in order to lift off the surface of the paper and reveal white marks for the blades and ears of grass.

Masking

A fine brush is needed to reserve individual blades of grass. The swaying motion of the river bank is followed with the strokes of masking fluid laid over subsequent washes of green.

1 Mask out a few grass stems with gestural strokes from a fine brush to determine the lay of the grass. Lay the first grass wash in cerulean and new gamboge.

2 When dry, mask out more grass blades by criss-crossing the other masking. Sponge in the distant trees.

3 Lay another greenish-gray wash, and when it dries, mask for a third time. With the last wash, push the dark tone into the base of the grasses.

4 Rub off all the masking and tint the untouched whites with a yellow ocher glaze, leaving the grass heads shimmering white.

Dry brush

Mix dry paint straight from the tube or pan. Drag your brush across to fill it with paint and then splay the hairs of the brush out into a fan shape. As you brush this across the paper, you will lay multiple lines of color.

3 Add yellow ocher in dry brush strokes and then use white gouache, straight from the tube, to draw down individual blades of grass with a fine brush.

1 First wash in the landscape to create a light base for the dry brushwork. Sap green is a useful grassy color.

4 Take the white blades across the dark reflections below the bank and the grass island.

2 Fill a size 4 brush with dark green paint and fan out the hairs. Brush the color onto the island of grass with upward strokes of the brush.

Harbors

The lively buzz of a fishing port, or boats

peacefully bobbing in a quiet bay, form the subject

of many fine watercolor paintings.

Try not to get too bogged down in small details; look for the main shapes so that you can convey the impression of the boats. Quick horizontal dashes of color will probably look more like distant yachts packed into a marina than hours spent carefully drawing every last deck and shackle.

Reserving white paper The essence of watercolor painting is the glow of transparent washes painted over white paper. Painting on rough paper is ideal for capturing the shimmering, dancing highlights of light on water. The pigment settles in the "troughs," leaving scattered highlights throughout the dried wash. The less wet the paint, the more effective the "tooth."

The sparkle of white yachts, masts, and reflections are most effectively delineated by leaving white paper. Reflections from white buildings also look fresher if created in this way. Lost highlights, such as masts, can be picked out in the final stages with opaque white paint.

Wax resist A light application of candle wax beneath washes will create a broken-color effect suggesting choppy water. It will "sit" only on the top of the paper grain, partially resisting the paint, which will settle unevenly. Wax could also be used over a rather too-uniform wash, with more color laid on top.

Wet-in-wet The reflections of boats can be painted by wetting the bottom of the hulls and the water below, dropping in a darker color and letting the paint run downward. If you want a definite waterline, dampen just the area below the hull, paint the color in along the waterline of the boat, and let it seep downward into the damp paper below. Use the same technique for the reflections of harbor walls and buildings.

Reserving white paper

The vibrancy of the white paper both under and between the colors is the secret of the freshness of watercolors. In this painting, experiment with a large 2-inch flat brush, without any preliminary drawing, to create a lively composition.

1 Lay the sky wash around the tops of the buildings. With the edge of the brush, block in the shadows of the buildings and the hull of the boat.

2 Draw the palm trees with the side of the brush and then use a finer brush to pick out the boat details, windows, and doors.

3 Brush in the reflection with bold strokes, remembering to leave areas of untouched paper to reflect the buildings. Strengthen the shadows and trees with a darker color.

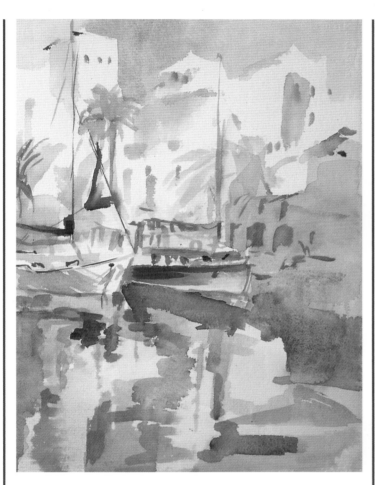

Wax resist

A white wax candle drawn in streaky movements over the light areas of a painting will quickly preserve exciting irregular highlights when covered with further washes.

1 Paint a light overall wash of yellow ocher. Block in the buildings loosely with Payne's gray. While the paint is wet, wax the left-hand side of the sky. When you paint another wash over this, a soft-edged streaky effect is created.

2 Wash yellow ocher over the waxed water and use a touch of burnt sienna in the middle distance. Mix Payne's gray and burnt sienna together to paint the silhouetted buildings and reflections.

4 Lay the palest of blue washes as a transparent glaze over the water to unify the reflection and to make it slightly darker than the image it reflects.

3 Pick out the masts, boats, and their reflections with the edge of the brush. With a limited palette, you can create a vibrant painting.

Hills

Hills have a strong emotive appeal, inviting you to explore what lies beyond, as well as creating a series of lovely and intriguing shapes.

Choose the time of day carefully, as the direction of the light changes the appearance of the hills. When the sun is overhead or directly in front, they will be flattened, with their forms hard to decipher. Oblique sunlight will cast shadows that describe the forms, while low sun, setting behind the hills, will silhouette them, allowing you to see them as simple shapes.

Wet-in-wet Softly rounded forms can be painted wet in wet. Drop darker color into the valleys before the wash has dried. If the paper is dry, dampen it beyond where you want the paint to run to ensure soft edges.

Create the structure of the hills by modeling from dark to light. Lighten the top of a rise and darken the dip beyond if you want the hill to stand out more.

To suggest an upward slope, dampen the paper above an imaginary line that represents the angle of the hill. Drop color into this along the slope line and let it extend softly upward into the damp paper. Clumps of grass and changes in surface created in this way will then also describe the lie of the land.

Glazes We recognize hills mainly by their contours. Draw the shapes carefully, either using a pencil first or going straight in with color, using the tip and edge of your brush as you lay the washes. Successive transparent washes (glazes) are an effective way of building up layers of overlapping hills.

Wet-in-wet

Be aware how damp your paper is as you lay each brushstroke into the preceding wet wash. Test it with the brush tip to see how far the paint spreads and wait if it spreads too far.

1 Paint a pale pink wash over all the paper, and darken it at the bottom. While wet, brush in the hills.

2 Use a warm, strong color in the foreground, letting it spread softly into the drying wash above.

3 Use small washes to describe the hill forms, working into them while they are wet, contrasting light against dark to separate the masses. With a small brush, draw directional lines into the hills while the paper is damp.

Glazes

Glazes are thin, transparent washes laid one over another. Leave the top of the previous wash exposed each time to create the advancing hills. The color of the top wash will be the sum of all the previous washes underneath.

2 Lay the background hill wash over this and follow this with another slightly darker wash of Hooker's green mixed with red.

1 With a large, flat ⅝-inch brush, lay an underwash of pale pink to provide a warm tone under the greens.

3 Lay additional glazes, making the middle-distance hills and foreground trees darker. For soft, crinkly edges, lay the next glaze just before the previous one dries.

4 Paint a dabbing wash of monestial green to describe the tree and shrubs, and with a lemon yellow wash, lay a final glaze over the sunlit leaves.

Islands

Simple but exciting paintings can be made by breaking an ocean horizon with the shape of an island, or silhouetting it against a sunset.

Or you can use an island as a compositional device to enliven a background. For distant islands use a one-touch wash with a well-filled brush to describe the whole shape. For small dotted islands, paint the form and the reflection with your first stroke or wash, then glaze over the reflection again to create the shoreline.

Graduated wash A strong simple statement is made by painting a graduated wash from sky to sea, leaving the area around the horizon as the lightest part. The island shape and its soft reflection then mark the horizon.

Wet-in-wet This is the perfect method for reflections of islands in still waters. Dampen the paper only below the island, using a tissue to dry any dampness on either side, as this would make the reflection spread horizontally. If you want the reflection to mirror the island precisely, apply the wash when the paper is nearly dry, as this gives you more control.

Reserving white paper To hint at white sand along a shoreline, reserve white paper in a narrow strip above the sea. Small white buildings on the shoreline can be suggested by reserving an irregular line of white paper.

Over a graduated wash/wet-in-wet

A simple sky/sea painting is transformed by the inclusion of the island. Use quick wet-in-wet brushstrokes made with a 2-inch household brush.

1 Lay a graduated wash of cyanine and ultramarine blue, darken the sea, and introduce green into the shallows.

2 Take a line of brown across the horizon as a base for the island. Blot out any excess water with a tissue.

3 Paint the island with a mix of yellow ocher and white gouache to give it substance. Drop undiluted white into the dark shadow areas of the fortress to increase opacity.

4 A simple dynamic painting has been achieved with relatively few brushstrokes.

2 Introduce yellow ocher into the distant mountains. Keep the sea very washy, and soften the tops of the distant hills with clear water.

3 Paint in the island in olive-green and ocher with a full brush, and lay it in strong diagonal strokes on the drying background.

One-touch brushstrokes

Again, a simple background sea/sky wash is laid and a dramatic island brushed into position with three simple strokes of a flat brush. Be bold and avoid the temptation to fiddle with the stroke after it is laid.

1 With a flat brush, paint a loose wash of cerulean, cobalt, and green. Wash out the clouds with clear water and blot with a tissue to retrieve the white paper.

4 As the color dries, touch more olive-green into the island peaks with the edge of the brush.

Lakes

There are few more appealing subjects than reflections in still water. Then a breeze comes up, ruffling the water surface, and the image is erased.

To make sure of a convincing reflection, it is best to paint, or at least to sketch in, the landscape first, so that you can match the reflection to the actual shapes. If the water is mainly light with dark reflections, leave it as blank paper initially. If there are light reflections in dark water, reserve white paper for the reflections and wash in the water early to preserve the unity of the painting. Or alternatively, use a dry brush or tissue to lift out the reflections from the color used for the water before the wash is dry.

Glazes Vertical washes of transparent color laid with a flat brush will create clean downward reflections. If you want to reserve a horizontal ripple line, mark it softly with pencil as a guide. Masking fluid could be used, but it may leave rather insensitive shapes.

To lay ripples over a wash, use thin horizontal glazes of diluted white gouache. This will create a glassy film which looks just like light reflected on water. Brush the paint on lightly and leave undisturbed.

Wet-in-wet For those lovely reflections that seem to blend into the water like curtains of chiffon, dampen the paper slightly and brush the color in below the shore line. Guide the flow of the paint by tilting your paper, then leave to dry before retouching.

If you have used plenty of pigment in the wash for the shore line, you can suck it down into the water with a slightly damp brush. Alternatively, use a dry brush to pull the wash down when it is still wet, or dampen the paper beneath the shore line and let the wet color spread. This technique is suitable if you wish to soften or lose the shore line.

Glazes/ opaque paint

With a size 6 round brush, overlay thin transparent washes of diluted paint to build up a shimmering scene of color. Use white gouache to draw in the ripples of the lake after the glazes are dry.

1 Block in diluted washes of Naples yellow, greens, and lilac in a generalized fashion. Use vertical strokes on the shoreline, contrasted with short diagonals in the foliage.

2 Paint glazes of thin color in patches over the dried washes. Darken the area below the waterline with a glaze of purple.

3 Draw in the ripples with white gouache. Use it fairly thickly; it will dry lighter than it appears when it is wet.

4 Strengthen the darks in the foreground to frame the background. The glazes create an almost stained-glass effect.

Wet-in-wet/ lifting out

Soft, runny reflections in watercolors are created by dropping the paint into a wet wash or by wetting the paper with clear water and then brushing in the paint. Always wet a wider area than you need to stop hard edges from developing when the color meets dry paper.

2 When dry, paint the dark shoreline silhouette. Dampen the paper under the lakeside down to the ocher, and leave a sliver of white paper to mark the edge. Brush the reflection gently into the damp area to mirror the shapes on the shore above.

3 Just before the reflection dries, lift out the horizontal ripples with a slightly damp brush. If the paint has dried already, rub the ripple with a damper brush or the edge of a tissue.

1 Using a size 11 round brush, paint in a pale Prussian blue sky onto dry paper, and brush yellow ocher and India red into it while wet. Wash the same color scheme into the lake.

4 When the paint is dry, brush in the reeds in indigo and Prussian blue, with single strokes for the leaves.

Mist

Hills or fields fading gradually into the mist, or a soft blanket turning trees into pale silhouettes— these seem like an invitation to paint.

They look easy, but are deceptively so, requiring thought, careful planning, and very little actual painting. Keep your palette of colors simple, avoiding bright hues and any strong contrasts of tone or hard lines—mist softens everything.

Wet-in-wet The most useful technique is the wet-in-wet wash. For an overall hazy appearance, the whole paper can be dampened so that the entire image is soft. For patches of mist, such as that rising from a river, the paper need only be dampened selectively. Objects seen through the mist can be painted in afterward when the paper is almost dry, using one-touch strokes so as not to disturb the wash.

To paint a landscape dissolving in misty layers, paint from back to front, building layer upon successive layer, patiently waiting for each to nearly dry before applying the next. Too wet and the color will run formlessly; too dry and the edges will be hard unless you are using very thin washes. Keep to one color, using progressively deeper tones.

Washing off This can be a troubleshooting method, but is also a technique in itself. If the color is too strong, or tones have too much contrast, wash the paint off with a large brush. You can even hold the painting under the faucet, but you must use a heavyweight paper (300 pound). Some colors will stain the paper, but these can be rubbed vigorously to give a wonderful old-leather look. If only one or two objects are at fault, lift some of the color off gently with a brush or corner of tissue.

White wash Another way of giving your image that misty feel is to use a large brush to drag a thin solution of white watercolor (Chinese white) gently over the painting—or you can apply it evenly with a sponge. Remember, the paint will dry less white than it looks when wet and will add a certain opacity to the painting.

Successive layers

With just one color, you can build up a misty landscape in layers. Let each wash dry before the next is painted. Do not alter the consistency of color—successive layers create the slightly darker tones.

1 Lay a wash of ultramarine and burnt sienna. When dry, brush in the distant ships, softening reflections with a clean damp brush.

2 Paint each layer over areas of the one before to build up a gradual deepening of tone.

3 Using small strokes, pick out darker features such as the hulls of boats, dock- sides, and windows in the warehouses.

Wet-in-wet

To create rising mist in the valleys, lay successive washes onto paper dampened only at the base of the wash. If a hard edge occurs, soften it before the paint dries with a brush full of clean water.

1 Dampen the paper in the valley areas of the painting. Brush in the color, allowing it to spread softly into the white paper at the bottom of each wash.

2 Paint each layer of hills into the white area, just before the previous wash dries. Touch in the tree forms in silhouette.

Opaque glaze

With a 2-inch flat brush, lay a glaze of semitransparent white gouache over a dry painting. Mix plenty of paint to an even, milky consistency.

1 Paint the landscape wet-in-wet, with bold playful strokes, letting the colors spread softly.

2 Overglaze with white gouache laid in horizontal stripes, allowing them to merge of their own accord. Use a tissue to lift out any area that picks up too much white.

3 Blot the darker trees before the white dries so that they appear to loom out of the mist. Avoid going over the painting too much or you will lift out the color.

Mountains

Few people can fail to be moved by the awesome majesty of mountain landscapes, and for the artist they provide a challenge and a thrill that no other subject can match.

Unless the mountains are flattened by mist or distance, it is important to establish their solidity. The low angle of the winter sun enhances their splendor by casting dramatic shadows, which also make it easier for the artist to paint convincingly three-dimensional forms.

After sketching in the mountain shapes, suggest their volume by means of cast shadows and shaded crevices. You can either begin with broad washes in a neutral tone, or go straight to your shadow colors, keying the rest of the painting to them.

You will also want to suggest their size, and you can give a sense of scale by including some familiar feature such as a person, climber's hut, or a group of houses nestling beneath the mountains.

Hard and soft edges The combination of hard and soft edges created by painting an area dampened in some parts only is very pleasing for a wild landscape. Evergreens can merge into each other at the bases, but if they are carefully drawn at the top, they look more interesting than starkly painted individual trees one against the other. Paint ledges and rocks with crisp edges, but let their bases merge into the mountainside wet-in-wet. Interesting textures for trodden snow can be created by scumbling.

Reserving white paper The beauty of snow scenes is that you don't have to do much painting to create an interesting image —a welcome relief when your hands are cold. Reserving white paper is the best way to "paint" white, with angular blue shadows describing the forms. For crisp white peaks, draw the shapes by taking the sky wash around them, using a large round brush with a good tip.

Hard and soft edges

Mixing washes without too much water allows you to work quickly on dried paint so that the brushstrokes remain hard-edged. Use clear water to soften hard-edged areas.

1 Paint the distant mountains over a damp, greenish sky wash. As the mountains come forward, lay linear brushstrokes over soft, dried washes.

2 Build the outline of the crags with single brushstrokes, describing the rocky slopes of the mountain. Paint a very wet wash of ocher for the foreground scree slope.

3 Scribble loose detail into the scree surface with the tip of the brush while the wash is wet. Dampen the base of the central mountain with clear water to make the colors spread softly.

Reserving white paper

It will help you to lay more confident shadow shapes if you sketch the mountain scene lightly to begin with. The untouched white paper is the strength and the freshness of the painting. Do not fiddle, and be certain of where the mountain shadows fall.

1 Paint a cobalt-blue sky, following the mountain ridge. While drying, use the same wash plus a little Payne's gray to paint in the shadow shapes of the mountain.

2 When dry, use light strokes of the same color, plus more Payne's gray, to create the surface variations, peaks, and ridges.

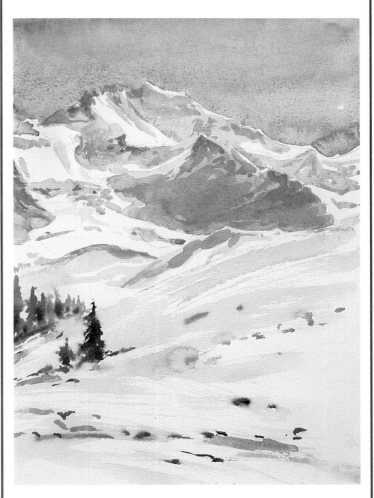

3 Into the pale wet wash on the mountain slope, drop small pools of cobalt blue and Payne's gray to show lumps of snow and ice. Dampen the paper slightly before drawing in the fir trees with downward strokes. Let them bleed softly.

Scumbling and masking

To scumble paint onto a surface, you should mix dry paint, fill the brush, and with a twisting, dabbing motion of the brush head, "grind" the paint onto the paper. Repeat the process for a delightfully varied texture.

1 Mask out the sharp edge of the mountain against the sky. Wet the paper, and lay a wash of Antwerp blue and Payne's gray. Where the color floods over the mountain top, lift it out with tissue.

2 Paint the mountain shadows with the same two colors. Scumble dry sepia, with twisting movements, onto the rocks and peppered snow in the center.

3 With a dilute but dry mixture of Antwerp blue and Payne's gray, scumble the trampled snow. Repeat, patting and twisting the brush head.

4 Remove the masking with the finger. Wet the white area and drop in Antwerp blue for soft shadows in the undulating snow.

Night

Even the smallest amount of light, whether natural or artificial, will break up the darkness to create exciting effects for the painter to try.

Moonlight shimmering on still water, street lights reflected from a lakeside road, the lit windows of houses against dark trees, or the last loom of light above hills as dusk succumbs to advancing night—all these would make promising subjects.

You will need to build up dark colors, so a wash all over the paper is a good way to start. Mix plenty of paint before you start, so that you do not get caught short, and make the wash darker at the top and bottom and lighter around the area broken by lights.

Reserving and masking Reserve white paper for bright areas such as the moon and its reflections, or for small pinpoints of light—distant street lights, for example—paint on little dots of masking fluid. Lay your dark washes boldly over the top, and, when they are dry, rub the masking fluid off very carefully. Touch in the colors of the lights with transparent dabs of yellow, red, and orange accordingly.

For the soft glow of moonlight on water, painting over wax resist breaks up the color to give a gentle, fluid reflection.

To create the haze you see around lights or around the moon, try using dry white gouache over the wash in a "scumbling" method, scrubbing it over the watercolor with a bristle brush. This will lighten the area around the light but some of the underlying color will show through. Alternatively use a sponge, dabbing the white on in layers. To tint the haze, use a dry color as well.

Masking and scumbling

For tiny lights, it is often easier to use masking fluid than to try to reserve the white paper. When the masking is removed, soften the hard edge by scumbling.

1 Mask out the streetlights and reflections. Wet the paper and lay a loose dark wash, leaving the area above the cottages untouched. Drop yellow ocher into this area and its reflection.

2 When dry, add the profile of the dark houses, softening the skyward edge by dropping clean water above the area to be painted and letting the indigo run into it.

3 Build up the darks, wash on wash. Rub off the masking and tint with diluted cadmium yellow. Scumble around the circle of the foreground light.

Reserving white paper

The untouched freshness of white paper is the brightest way to create lights in watercolor. Wet the paper all over, but as you do, draw around the moon and down each side of the reflection, so that those parts of the paper remain dry.

1 Flood a rich mixture of indigo and ultramarine blue into the dampened paper, helping it around the moon with the brush and coaxing little ripples across the reflection.

2 While damp, add the horizon feature in deep indigo, letting it spread into the sky and water.

3 Sketch the pier and its mirrored reflection with dark strokes over dry paint. Dampen and blot the reflection.

4 Touch in the boats with indigo using the tip of the brush. Where the fore-ground crosses the moon's reflection, exchange the indigo for red and ocher.

Lifting out and opaque white

Soft lights can be retrieved while a wash is still damp by lifting out the color with a clean brush or tissue. If the paint has dried, it will need rubbing with a damp brush. For larger areas "massage" the area with a clean, damp sponge.

1 Lay a pale pink wash, leaving the moonlit surfaces as white paper. Block in the dark areas with an underwash of Payne's gray, monestial blue, and ultramarine.

2 Strengthen the dark areas, working wet-in-wet and wet-on-dry. Lay a dark wash over the sky.

3 Before the sky wash dries, lift out the moon and its halo with a clean, slightly damp brush to reveal the pinkish wash underneath.

4 Add white to restore the luminosity of the moon, and rub it with your finger softly around the edge of the moon in order to create the halo.

5 When dark color dries, it may appear dull. A brushload of pure ultramarine will create vibrant color in the shadow of the house and nearby bushes.

Panoramas

Often a sketchbook page will seem too small to capture the awe-inspiring effect of a panoramic view stretching around you on all sides.

So why not change your format? Either open your sketchbook and paint across a double-page spread, or crop your paper to make an elongated rectangle. You will find that the composition immediately begins to fall into place.

Wash in the sky and distant landscape with broad, free strokes. Try to "feel" the sweep of the land, and let your brushstrokes suggest the twists and turns in the contours of hills and valleys, rivers, and roads.

Brushwork Build up the landscape with graduated washes and overlaid brushstrokes, using the shape of the brush to describe forms. A flat brush is useful here; have a look at some of Cézanne's watercolors of Mont St. Victoire, in which he used short, flat brushstrokes of transparent color right across the valley floor to the foot of the mountain. Horizontal and vertical strokes can suggest fields, houses, roofs, and trees. More precise detail can be added later, or you may find that the brushmarks have established your view quite satisfactorily.

Wet-in-wet Soft, rounded forms such as trees and bushes can be indicated by small wet-in-wet blobs. Touch in the color along the lines of roads, rivers, or hedges to anchor them to the earth, and let the color spread upward in soft, irregular shapes. You can model these forms while still wet, with more drops of color, or add more color wet on dry.

Overlaid brushstrokes

Delicate lightweight brushstrokes, together with small glazes laid one upon the other, make up a quick interpretation of an enormous subject. Keep your paint solutions on the drier side to enable you to paint quickly over dried brushstrokes.

1 Use the shadows to draw the structure of the range of hills with a neutral color.

2 Build up the mountain shapes with small directional brushstrokes. Wash in the valley with a loose narrowing zigzag, and suggest details with the tip of the brush to create a sense of distance and scale.

3 Darken the foreground to frame the valley and lay blobby brushstrokes to mark the trees, enlarging them as they come closer.

Wet-in-wet

Use a large 2-inch flat brush on damp paper to create the broad sweeps of the land without getting bogged down in detail. Change to a smaller brush to hint at details with small, persuasive brushmarks open to free interpretation.

1 Lay a variegated wash of cerulean and pink over wet paper. When almost dry, brush in the flat-topped mountain with cerulean and raw umber, testing the dampness with the tip of the brush before you lay the wash.

2 Paint small directional brushstrokes into wet washes across the middle distance to vaguely describe the lie of fields, hedges, etc. Drop darker color into the wet paint for the foreground tree.

4 Create the swerve of the road with a sweep of Naples yellow. Hint at trees and bushes with simple directional brushstrokes, using stronger tones in the foreground.

3 As the wash dries on the mountain, draw in linear details with dryish paint. Mix a little red and ocher with white to create a pinkish color in the middle distance.

Pathways

A path winding off into the unknown evokes a sense of mystery. Someone looking at your painting will wonder where it goes or what is around the bend.

However quickly you make your preliminary drawing, whether with pencil or brush, concentrate on the perspective of the pathway as it runs away from you.

Whether a pathway is bordered by flowers, trees, or bushes, shadows cast across it will always help to create interest and establish its horizontal surface. A leafy shadow falling across the track will also help to pull the foreground toward you. Even if there is no direct sunlight, breaking the surface with different tones will make it more interesting, or you can introduce features such as scattered stones to create foreground interest. Close-up features framing the pathway across the front of the picture plane "invite" the viewer into the picture, to seek out vines, branches, leaves, and flowers that you can use in this way.

Spattering/flicking Spattering or flicking paint along the surface of the pathway will enliven a dull wash. Use the colors already in your painting, so that the spatter does not look too obtrusive, and encourage larger blobs of paint to fall in the foreground and smaller ones in the background as the path recedes.

Hard and soft edges Both the borders and the pathway itself will benefit from a mixture of hard and soft edges. Break border lines with an occasional soft edge, either by dampening the paper in places before you lay your wash or by lifting out with a damp brush or sponge later. Let flowers or foliage bordering the path fall freely across the line of the pathway to make its linear shape less regular.

Spatter/flicking

Mix liquid solutions of paint in the palette. Dip an old toothbrush into the color and hold it across the area to be spattered. Pull back across the brushhead with the end of a paintbrush, releasing the speckles over the paper.

1 Lay the basic composition with loose warm washes, reserving the line of the pathway.

2 Protect the rest of the painting with paper, and spatter the triangle of pathway with burnt sienna sprayed from the toothbrush. Flick larger blobs of ocher from the head of a loaded paintbrush by tapping the end. Peel back the protective paper to reveal the spattered pathway.

3 Remove the protective paper and flick some burnt umber and some clean water onto the pathway.

4 The burnt umber merges with the water and softens the spotty pathway. Define the border of the path with grasses.

Hard and soft edges

Drop liquid color from the tip of the brush into wet washes to create soft, merging colors. Alternate with brushstrokes and small washes painted over dried paint to form a contrast of edges.

1 Draw the composition with a light yellow wash. While wet, draw in viridian brushstrokes and let the colors spread. Paint a warm pink wash over the pathway.

2 When nearly dry, build up different-color washes of light violet, light green, and cadmium red on the flower borders. Let them merge wet in wet, marking the pathway with soft edges.

3 Wash in the trees and dot in blobs of yellow while the paint is wet. Lay a shadow wash across the path, with a similar color on the tree trunks.

4 Lay a deeper wash of ultramarine and permanent rose over the shadows, dropping ultramarine into the wet wash to vary the tone. With short linear strokes, define the foliage in the foreground.

People

A figure in a landscape will immediately attract attention, so try to paint it well, or it could spoil the whole effect.

The secret is to treat the figure in the same manner as the rest of the painting; overworking it or giving it too much detail will make it stick out like a sore thumb. If you are unsure about the scale, cut a little figure out of low-tack masking tape, wash over it in the color you will be using, and move it around gently into the position you think is right. Then draw lightly around it, marking the top and bottom, and remove.

Once the size is correct in relation to the painting, decide what the overall shape of the figure is. Practice painting figure silhouettes from life, and keep them on hand. If you are painting a view with a figure which moves before you have finished, you will have a record of a similar shape which you can add to the painting when you wish.

One-touch brushstrokes One-touch brushstrokes to indicate a figure's stance are the most lively, but they take practice and courage. The artist, Ian King, teaches his students to paint an "M" over a "W," topped with a small blob for the head, to create effective standing or walking figures; this is a very handy formula. Color for clothing can be painted either in the initial strokes or brushed in later to retain the overall tone. Touch in small highlights with white paint.

Back views and hats are a great help, eliminating the need to paint faces—which attract the eye even more than the overall figure. If you need to indicate facial features, keep them to simple shadows for the indentations of the face.

Reserving white paper The highlights on a figure's clothing help to describe the forms of the body beneath. Carefully mark these highlit shapes when sketching your figure and try to reserve the white paper by painting crisply around them.

Figure silhouettes

With very quick, dryish brushstrokes, believable figures can be swiftly painted in action. Lively, imprecise lines look more alive than rigid, carefully drawn people. Gesture is important; look for shape. Your people don't have to be accurate to be effective.

1 Lay a pale wash for the sky and wash in the trees while wet. Leave the snowy hill as white paper. Sketch the figures in lightly in gray with a brush, and emphasize movement with the brushmark.

2 As the color dries, paint a dash of color into a couple of figures for variation. Now go over them with a darker color, but leave some of the undertone peeping through.

3 Strengthen the background trees slightly against the figures, and brush in the foreground tree.

The figures are lively and descriptive with very little painting.

One-touch brushstrokes

In this example use a quick touch of white gouache to indicate the body of the man walking his dogs. For the white to stand out, a dark background is necessary. The head and legs are, likewise, quick strokes of the brush.

1 Wash in the beach landscape with a large flat brush, wet-in-wet. Let the colors spread gently, but guard against losing the horizontal stripe of the sea.

2 Darken the shoreline with sideways strokes before the background dries. Brush in the foreground grasses with a size 10 round brush, using Naples yellow and white.

3 Paint the figure and dogs with thick white gouache paint on the tip of the brush. Add a dark blob for the head, and quick downward strokes for the legs, on the slightly damp wash.

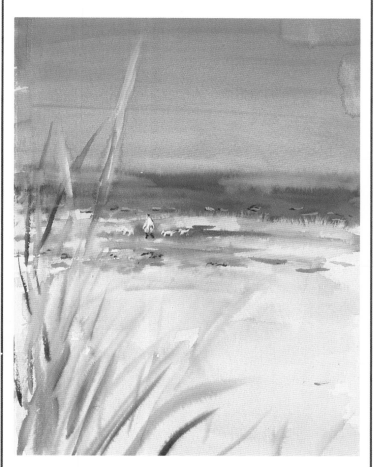

4 Hint at the face with the tiniest dash of burnt sienna and white, and use dark dashes for the hands. Note how the addition of the figures makes the painting come alive – it now tells a story.

Reserving white paper

To retain the fresh highlights of untouched white paper, a sketch of the body shapes before you start may be necessary. Then you can confidently "draw" the paint around the shapes without hesitant breaks in the wash.

3 With the tip of the brush and a strong dark color, paint the shadows along the shaded sides of the limbs and faces.

1 Wash in a basic background wash of cerulean and yellow ocher around the highlights of the figures.

2 Paint the shadows on the clothes as you build up the general tonal play of the painting. Think of the figures as part of the landscape.

4 Where local color is needed on the standing woman's clothes, use a diluted glaze of orange. Stronger color is used on the washing. Erase any pencil lines that obscure the freshness of the white paper.

Rain

Blurred images and puddled reflections may not sound much fun, but watercolor paintings of rain are a pleasure to paint and a delight to behold.

While rain is falling, objects become blurred, so you want the soft effect created by wet-in-wet washes, working either with one continual wash, or with successive layers of wet-in-wet. Rain is a marvelous excuse for running the colors of different objects into one another. Soft reflections in wet paths or roads can be dropped in before the wash is dry.

Painting a rainbow Setting a rainbow in landscape successfully is tricky, but one way to do it is to start by lifting the color out of the sky wash, making an arc shape with a damp sponge. You can then paint in the colors while the area is still damp, to produce soft gradations. To shine in a painting, the rainbow must be considerably lighter than everything else, so if the sky above is light, use artistic license and make it darker.

Reserving white paper After rain the landscape glistens, with shiny highlights everywhere. The secret of painting the shimmering light of puddles, wet leaves, and so on is to reserve white paper. These must be the lightest parts of the painting, so any other whites need to be toned down with a pale wash to allow them to shine out. The reflections of objects in puddles are usually still and are best painted with well-defined transparent washes broken up by white-paper highlights.

Masking with a pen To suggest streaks of rain in the foreground, use masking fluid applied with a pen, which will give really fine strokes. Draw them along a ruler to help you maintain a direction. If they look too obvious when the masking is removed, wash over them with a pale uneven wash.

Rainbow – lifting out

The lifting-out technique can be used to soften edges, diffuse and modify color, and also to create highlights. Paint can be lifted out using a dampened sponge, although the success of this method depends on the color to be lifted and the type of paper you choose. Bockingford, Saunders, and Cotman papers are all excellent.

1 Lay an overall wash of purple-gray, and lift out the arc of the rainbow with a sponge while still wet.

2 While the arc is still damp from the lifted wash, paint in the colors of the rainbow in bands. Paint red, then yellow, encouraging orange to be created by their merging. Likewise, paint cerulean blue next to yellow; green will be created by their merging. Finally, paint violet next to the blue.

3 Create a sideways light on the land as the sun shines across the landscape onto the dark clouds.

Reserving white paper

Although the puddle on the dry ground is reserved with white paper, because the still water mirrors the sky, it may in fact have to be painted darker in parts than the landscape itself. Contrast dark against light and light against dark at the edges of the puddle.

1 Wet the area of the sky and land, reserving white paper for the puddle. Brush in a vigorous variegated wash of ocher, light red, Prussian blue, and burnt umber.

2 Take light red and ocher across the landscape and around the puddle. While wet, drop touches of sap green into the base of wash bands and let them spread upward to form clumps of soft grass.

3 Paint the horizon details slightly darker than the rain cloud. Use the side of the tip of the brush to paint non-specific tree shapes and trunks.

4 Draw the dead trees against the sky with the tip of the brush. Wash into the puddle the mirrored tone of the sky, letting the darker color run to the bottom.

5 As the water wash dries, draw down the tree reflections in soft-edged, straight, or wiggly lines.

6 Darken the clumps of grass by wetting the paper and dropping in more color with the tip of the brush.

To make the water look wetter, touch in the reflections of the grasses in the puddle.

Wet-in-wet

Wet all the paper so the underwashes are soft. Flood your colors into gradually drying paper so that the background trees only spread very slightly compared with the foreground greens. Make greens more gray with a touch of alizarin crimson.

1 Lay a Prussian blue wash, wet-in-wet, leaving the roadway untouched. Drop differing greens into the Prussian blue wash.

2 Describe the Landrover with dark specific shapes. Draw in the reflection of the vehicle on dry paper, leaving white spaces between the broken strokes.

3 Touch in the luggage and the passengers. Paint the zebras crossing the road in a mid-gray tone with the side of the tip of the brush (i.e. block them rather than filling them in).

4 Paint the foreground tree trunk, draw in the zebras' stripes with white gouache, and darken the manes with gray. No prizes for guessing the title of the painting!

Rivers and Streams

Water in movement makes an enticing watercolor subject, whether it is a wide, peaceful river flowing gently through meadows or a busy brook cascading down hills or racing around rocks.

Painting water requires planning. It is important not to over-work the paint. Work out the composition so that you know exactly where you want to reserve white paper.

Tone and color Contrast of tone is essential to suggest the depth and transparency of water. Dark reflections with light ripples of reserved white paper will help to establish the surface. Pay attention to perspective; the narrowing of a river running away from you will create depth in the painting. Use stronger foreground tones and paler tones in the distance.

Look at color carefully also. Some parts of a river may reflect the blue of a sky, but never assume water is blue; you will see wide color variations depending on reflections, the play of light, and what lies on the river or stream bed.

Wet-in-wet Dissolving color wet-in-wet is the ideal technique for reflections. Mix up strong solutions of color for the dark, shaded reflections under the banks, and allow backruns and other chance watercolor effects to add life.

For clumps of grass and gently sloping river banks, dampen the paper above the river's edge and drop color in at the water-line, letting it spread softly upward.

Wax resist To suggest flow lines in the water, or a surface ruffled by wind, wax resist is a useful technique. Draw the flow of the river with a candle. When you paint over it, the watercolor sticks only to the unwaxed areas, looking like sparkling water.

Masking You can create subtle running-water effects by half rubbing off your masking fluid, or scuffing it directionally. Several layers can be built up, with more fluid removed before each wash.

Overhanging reeds and grasses can be masked out to keep them light against a dark wash. The ripple of the waterline can also be reserved in this way.

Wax resist

Use an ordinary candle to lay wax over light washes. Additional paint will not stick to the waxed areas, so you can freely wash darker tones over the top. Exciting textures are created by the paint globules drying over the wax.

1 Paint a washy background of greens and blues, leaving the passage of the river and the sky lighter than the rest.

2 Lay wax quite strongly over the center of the river and the parts of the foliage you wish to keep light.

3 Paint more washes right across the waxed areas and the rest of the painting. When dry, apply more wax on the water to hold the mid-tone.

3 Scuff the masking again so that more of the paper is exposed, and wash over it with a glaze of diluted blue. Paint in the shaded sides of the trees and rocks.

4 Paint strong dark color over the wax to pull the trees and their reflections together.

Scuffed masking

With a kneaded eraser, rub and scuff the dry masking in on itself so that it pulls away in rubbery strands but is not removed. Paint over the masking and repeat the process several times to create a "marbling" effect.

1 Mask over the white water. When the fluid is dry, scuff the masking in the direction of the river's flow.

2 Paint Prussian blue over the masking, pushing it well into the hollows of white paper between the strands of scuffed masking. Brush in the distant trees.

4 Rub off the masking completely when dry and paint pale directional brushstrokes to emphasize the flow of the river. Strengthen the rocks and trees.

Roads

Roads snaking over hills or running straight over flat plains create a focus for the eye, and help to define the forms of the landscape.

When you first sketch a road, do so without looking down at the paper, letting your pencil or brushline follow its flow. The fluidity of that first line will keep the painting alive.

Shadows cast across the road by trees and other objects are a great help in defining the flat surface. Lighten the shadows as they recede. A shadowy foreground cast by the leaves of an overhanging tree will enliven a dull foreground and enhance the perspective effect.

An overall underwash that encompasses both the road and the landscape bounding the road will keep the painting unified in color. Paint the surface of the road horizontally rather than vertically so that you can strengthen the bands of color as you come forward and vary the surface wash.

Bodycolor If you find that the edge of the road is too monotonous, break it up by painting overhanging grasses with opaque bodycolor (gouache). Darken the shadows underneath to create depth. White bodycolor can also be used to paint in road markings. Any of these devices, or a road sign, can create an interesting focal point.

Lifting out If the road is rolling over hills, the crests will be lighter than the hollows. Use a damp brush or sponge to lift out the color in these areas, and soften any sharp delineations between the road and the verge in the same way.

For the impression of a distant road running through the landscape, wet a brush, sponge, or paper towel and lift out the color from the landscape, rubbing firmly in the direction of the road's flow. If you wish to tint it, wait until the paper is thoroughly dry.

Bodycolor

Mixing white paint (either gouache or watercolor) with watercolor pigments increases opacity. Overlaying glazes of these semi-translucent colors gives solidity, and a matte effect ideal for this dry desert road.

1 Mix a little white gouache with the colors used to lay the washes. Use the brush side to make horizontal and vertical marks. Scratch off paint on the distant road for a broken highlight.

2 For the scrubby landscape, pat small patches of white paint over the darker wash on the left-hand side. Use streaks of white down the length of the road to help create perspective.

3 A little spattering and smudging creates foreground interest. Pick out the distant hills with a few dark brushstrokes.

Lifting out

Tissues, dry brushes, sponges, and blotting paper can be used for lifting out color from a wash before it dries. A soft-edged light is created in this way. Some colors do, however, stain the paper; others, if you mop them immediately, will lift out completely. A tissue will pick up more color than a brush.

1 Lay an overall wash of yellow ocher. Lift out the distant road with a tissue, and the foreground road with a large dry brush, thus retaining a little more of the color in the foreground.

2 Block in the main color washes of the painting, reserving the underwash of ocher for the rocks and tree trunks.

3 Drag dry paint across the surface of the road, using it to describe the camber. Emphasize the bend in the road with dry, longitudinal brushmarks.

4 Spatter some speckles of color into the foreground. When dry, flick some color onto the area and move it around with a dry brush. While still damp, lift out the "wheel" marks to emphasize the sweep of the road.

5 Pick out the birch trees with white gouache. Touch in the branches with the tip of the brush.

Rocks

The varied shapes, forms, and textures of rocks offer a wealth of possibilities. Once you have established the structures, you can have fun experimenting with texture.

Brush in the main dark areas with a neutral tone, looking carefully at the shapes they make, as these describe the three-dimensional forms. If the rocks are gently rounded, further washes can be applied wet into wet, but for angular forms you need crisp, hard edges, so wait until each wash is dry and build up the forms in successive planes. Keep it simple initially: select three tones from pale to dark and build the structure of the rocks with these. If the rocks have an overall pinkish tinge, this color could be used for the first wash.

Wet-in-wet Working wet-in-wet on individual rocks and boulders will create exciting textures. Once you have achieved an effect you like, wait for the area to dry before adding more color; if you disturb the surface too much while it is still damp, your painting will lose its freshness.

Texture methods Crystals of sea salt sprinkled into wet paint make a fascinating patina that imitates lichen-covered rocks (see CLIFFS).

Painting over wax—candle or white wax crayon—creates another texture suitable for weathered rock (see BUILDINGS), and you can make the paint behave in interesting ways by laying other water-repellent substances, such as turpentine or oil on the paper under a wash.

Sponging paint onto the paper is a quick and easy way to liven up the surface and suggest texture, and for more random effects, blobs of color can be flicked on; this is a useful way to introduce other colors in an irregular way.

Further Information
☞
Cliffs, page 38.
Buildings, page 35.

Variegated wash

Merge colors, wet-in-wet, to create an underpainting. While the variegated wash is wet, color can be dropped in. The structure of the rocks is drawn on top, and the rocks take on individual colors in a total harmony.

1 Sketch the rocks and lay a washy mixture of viridian, mauve, India red, and ultramarine. Drop and flick more color into the wet wash.

2 With line and small washes of indigo, itemize the individual rocks and the gaps between them.

3 Use brushstrokes of white gouache to pick out light ridges and faces on the angular rocks. The rocks tumble together as a whole, but appear to have been painted in different colors.

Wet-in-wet/ sponging/spatter

Create rotund forms by dropping color into the shaded sides of wet washes on the rocks. Once the structure is realized, surface textures can be overlaid by applying dry paint with a sponge and spattering paint from a toothbrush.

3 | Cut the boulder shape out of tracing paper. Fill an old toothbrush with dark paint and spatter the paint from it across the rock surface from one corner.

1 | Sketch the landscape. Lay your washes to build up the tonal structure of the composition. Drop indigo into the wet, shaded sides of rocks, allowing it to spread.

4 | Apply paint with a sponge to the dark foreground rocks and, with wetter paint, pat it onto the middle-distance rocks for a softer effect.

2 | Having established the lights and darks of the rocks, sponge indigo across the edges of light as if the grainy surface were turning away from the light and casting small shadows.

Salt crystals

Painting the rocks wet-in-wet, but creating the texture by scattering salt crystals into the wet washes, gives a similar subject a totally different look. The crystals soak up the pigment from the wash and leave a gentle patina on the surface.

4 When dry, dust off the salt. Lay a wet wash of darker color into the shaded areas and scatter more crystals into the wet paint.

1 Block in the shadows of the rocks with blue, and wash in yellow ocher while wet. Let them merge.

2 Scatter crystals of salt over the rock surface while still very wet.

3 You can actually watch the color separating away from the crystals as the pigment is absorbed by the salt.

5 Dust the crystals off when they are dry and touch in the little boy playing in the sand to suggest scale.

Seas

The sea—relentlessly pounding on a stony shore or gently lapping over bleached sands—is a highly evocative subject; a good seascape is a painting to treasure.

The movement of water is tricky to paint unless you understand it, so spend some time watching the sea. Divide your sketchbook page into four and sketch or paint the life of a wave as it rises, curls into a crest, breaks upon the shore, and then backwashes toward a new wave to repeat the process. You will begin to see a pattern, and, when you plan your picture, you will be able to decide at which state of formation you want to paint a wave. You will be surprised at how much you can paint from memory.

When you paint, use your brushstrokes to imitate the movement of the sea, making long horizontal strokes for distant waves, and short, triangular peaked strokes for the closer ones.

Variegated and graduated washes If you paint the sea and the sky using a graduated or variegated wash, dampen your paper only down to the crests of the waves. The wash will stop at the dry paper, leaving a crisp edge. Continue your wash under the froth with darker transparent color, lighten it across the sand, and break it with bands of white spume. Using a rough paper will leave small flecks of white showing to suggest "white horses" in the distance.

Spattering/scratching To paint the plumes of spray thrown up by the sea as it crashes against rocks, spatter masking fluid from a toothbrush onto the area at the outset. When you rub it off at the end, use a little tone to suggest three-dimensions within the white spray. Alternatively, spatter white paint over your washes; it will also sink into the darker washes slightly, providing varieties of tone.

The spume of broken waves can be created by scratching off dry color with the side of a blade, and small flecks of foam and lines of spray can be lifted out with the point of a scalpel.

Graduated wash

Mix plenty of color in the palette and, laying your wash in horizontal strokes, gradually lighten it by adding water to your color as you go down the page. To darken the whole graduated wash, wait for it to dry before painting gently over it in the same way.

1 Wet the paper and lay a graduated wash of ultramarine and cobalt violet down to the crest of the wave. Drag dry paint in under the breaking waves.

2 Draw darker shadow lines under the crests and wash in the shoreline.

3 Take a wash of darker color along the horizon and into the distant sea. Strengthen the sky with another graduated wash to balance it with the dark horizon.

Variegated wash

Use a selection of earth colors, merging wet-in-wet as a variegated wash for the sky and sea: yellow ocher, India red, burnt umber, Prussian blue, and indigo.

4 | Describe the boat with two tones and sketch in the reflection in the sand with dry, horizontal strokes.

1 | Wet the sky down to the crest of the wave and drop in a variety of earth colors to create a brooding sky and a dark sea. Repeat the colors of the sky in the wet shoreline.

5 | Pick out the silhouettes of the men with well-loaded, one-touch brushstrokes of undiluted indigo. Darken the rising wave with the same color and strengthen the shoreline reflection to match the sky.

2 | Mark the distant waves with horizontal washes of indigo. Wash ocher and Prussian blue under the arching wave.

3 | Use dry brushstrokes to suggest the curve of the wave as it tumbles over, making them darker as they reach the broken spume at the base of the wave.

Spatter/ scratching off

White foam can be restored or created by spattering thick white paint from the head of a flat brush or a bristle brush. Scratch off the surface of the paper to reveal the pure white paper underneath a painted area so that you can create streaks of windblown surf.

3 | Spatter thick white gouache from the head of a full brush. Spatter the paint from one point to give a pivotal direction to the spume.

1 | Brush the dark underside of a crashing wave into a damp, greenish wash.

4 | Scratch off the painted surface of the paper on the turning crest of the wave in an upward, diagonal direction. Darken under the curl of the wave with undiluted Payne's gray.

2 | Create dynamic movement in the tumbling surf by vigorously scratching with a knife and brushing across the wet paint.

Skies

The sky is the light source for the land, so the two are inseparable. But even on their own, skies make great paintings, with just a touch of foreground to link them to the earth.

Ultramarine, or a mixture of cobalt blue and ultramarine, would be suitable for tropical or Mediterranean landscapes, while cerulean and Prussian blue are cooler blues ideal for the temperate zones. Cobalt blue makes a cheerful blue sky.

Look carefully at cloud colors also; at certain times of day there is a good deal of yellow and brown among the grays and near-whites. Ultramarine and burnt sienna mixed together make a warm gray for the shadowy parts of clouds, but there are no recipes for cloud colors, since they vary widely. Try different colors, linking sky to landscape.

Washes For a clear blue sky, the graduated wash is the perfect technique. Dampen the paper and brush in stronger color at the top. Use a large brush and tilt the paper to help the paint flow smoothly. Absorb pools of water at the sides and bottom with corners of a paper towel.

Skies of several colors, especially stormy skies, are effectively painted with a variegated wash (see STORMS). For the effect of sheets of rain or shafts of sun, dampen the whole sky area, paint a band of color along the top, and tilt the paper to encourage the color to run downward in soft streaks.

Wet-in-wet This is a superb technique for painting panoramic skies. A little control is necessary to make sure that the tops of clouds are hard-edged on dry paper and the bases softened with wet-in-wet washes (see CLOUDS).

Further Information
☞
Clouds, page 40.
Storms, page 104.

Graduated wash

Stretch the paper and prepare plenty of color before you begin. Use a size 12 round brush or a large flat brush to lay the wash in horizontal strips. Gradually dilute the paint as the wash is applied.

1 As you lay the strips of color, let them merge with each other without over-painting the previous strip, and dilute the color as you go.

2 With a size 7 brush, paint the landscape washes over the dried sky wash. The red-orange landscape contrasts well with the Antwerp blue of the sky.

3 Lay another wash of darker color for the central massif and mark in the shadows.

4 ▎ Pick out the shadows in the landscape features so they stand out well against the light horizon.

2 ▎ Paint the sky in big, sweeping curves on dampened paper, tilting the board so the color runs in a diagonal direction.

3 ▎ When dry, wet the clouds again and paint another streaky wash, now tilting the paper downward so that the color settles in the base of the clouds.

Tilting/lifting out (cloud and sun effects)

Tilt the board as you lay the cloud washes to create a flowing movement to the clouds. Lift out the sunbeams with a dry brush while the paint is wet. Lift out the sky above the hills with the rubbing movement of a damp brush.

1 ▎ Turn a graduated wash upside-down so the darker color is at the bottom. Mask the shoreline and wash in the hills. Lift out the sunbeams while wet with a dry brush.

4 ▎ Lift out the color behind the darkened hills with a damp brush, and dry-brush the color onto the sparkling sea.

Snow

Snow transforms a familiar landscape with white carpets and branches of trees outlined in white to create a magical filigree effect.

The best way to paint snow—or rather not to paint it—is to leave it as white paper, using the shapes of the shadows or undulations to describe the forms of the landscape. Reserve the white paper generously; it can always be painted over later, but it cannot easily be restored. Be inventive with shadows: blues that granulate, such as ultramarine and cerulean, make interesting textures, while cobalt blue is a clean fresh color ideal for the luminous shadows caused by reflection from a blue sky.

Wet-in-wet A thick covering of snow softens the forms, so to paint the soft rounded shapes, work your shadows wet-in-wet. Dampen the area well beyond the reach of the shadow so that no hard edge develops from the spreading wash. Use small touches of wet-in-wet shading around features half-buried in the snow to suggest the thickness of the blanket around them. Drifts of snow can be shown by hollows on the leeward side.

Masking/spattering For lines of snow resting on fences and branches, use masking fluid, and, when you remove it, suggest the thickness of the snow by a narrow band of wet-in-wet shadow washed along the bottom edge. Falling snow reserved with masking fluid looks a little too obvious, so instead, spatter white paint in a controlled manner from the top of the sky downward. To render a wild blizzard, direct the spatter diagonally or horizontally across the page.

Reserving white paper/wet-in-wet

A lightly brushed sketch in pale gray will allow you to lay the washes boldly and still reserve plenty of white paper for the snow. Soften the landscape by blobbing the color into wet washes.

1 Lay a warm sky wash around the tree shapes and above the ground. Start to build up the foliage with wet, gray-green, blobby washes.

2 Paint the shadows on the snow with cobalt blue. Encourage the color to settle in the base of the wash by tilting the board.

3 Wash in patches of warm mauve and gray for the winter trees. When dry, pick out the branches with the tip of the brush in lively strokes. Add a few intriguing footprints!

Masking and spatter

Use masking fluid to reserve white paper for the snow on the branches. Dip a toothbrush in white gouache mixed to a creamy consistency, hold it face down ½ to 1 inch above the painting and release speckles of paint by pulling your finger swiftly back across the bristles.

3 Darken the tree, using dry brushwork at the base. Spatter thick white gouache over the top half of the painting with the toothbrush.

1 Sketch the tree form in light gray. Mask the snow-laden branches. Lay a streaky wash of ocher and light red over the sky and let it dry.

2 Dampen the sky and wash a mix of light red and cobalt blue over in streaks. Dampen the snow and use the same wash to draw in undulating shadows.

4 Rub off the masking fluid to reveal snow-laden branches. One wonderful wintry painting!

Storms

The tumultuous sky at the height of a storm, rain-drenched trees swaying under the force of the wind —these are exciting to watch and paint.

Storms are energetic, so try to suggest movement with agitated brushstrokes, or work wet-in-wet to convey the dynamism of clouds moving across the darkened sky.

Variegated wash Stormy skies shift and change with the speed of the wind, so a variegated wash is ideal, as the colors themselves move as you lay them. You need to work carefully to prevent a blurred muddle. Choose colors which will provide lights and darks and retain light passages between the dark clouds to create depth. A useful palette might be diluted raw sienna for the lights, and mixtures of burnt umber, India red, Prussian blue, and indigo for the darks.

If the dark parts are drying too light, drop more pigment in while the wash is still wet. Blooms and backruns that develop may enhance the effect, but if they don't look right, leave the wash to dry and lift out unwanted edges with a damp brush.

Lifting/scratching out To lighten clouds or suggest sunbeams, use a tissue or dry brush to lift out color while the wash is drying. You will probably need to do this several times, as the wet color will seep back into the shaft of light (see SKIES).

Trees and foliage may be dark in the foreground and softly lit in the middle distance. This effect can also be created by lifting out with a tissue or sponge. Lightning streaks can be scratched out with a fine blade.

Further Information
☞
Skies, page 100.

Variegated wash

This variegated wash is laid on dry paper to maintain control of the light areas between the storm-clouds until softening them at the end with opaque white. Strong dark colors are dropped into wet washes and allowed to spread.

1 Mark the outline of the buildings with blue-gray. Boldly wash in the clouds with a size 10 round sable brush, leaving white lights in between.

2 Paint a yellow wash into some of the light areas and drop darker color into the cloud bases, wet-in-wet. Strengthen the urban landscape below.

3 Use white bodycolor to create semitranslucent light areas between the clouds. Dab and blot freely throughout the painting, if required.

Scratching out

Use the side of a single-edged razor-blade to scratch out the flashes of lightning from a dark stormy sky. The darker the background, the brighter the revealed paper will appear. Use a heavy paper.

3 Brush in the foreground grasses. Make sure the paper is completely dry before scratching out the streaks of lightning with the edge of the razor-blade.

1 Lay a wash of Antwerp blue. Mask the shoreline with tape. Wet the sky area and flood in big sweeps of Payne's gray. Let it dry, and strengthen it in the same way.

4 Be firm with the blade in order to reveal good, clear, white lines against the dark stormy sky.

2 Paint the dark hills and create the sparkling water by dragging dry paint across in horizontal streaks.

Sunlight and Shadows

There is probably no subject quite as appealing as sunlight and shadow, and it is most pleasant to paint outside on a warm, sunny day under the shade of a tree.

Look carefully at the colors of shadows. They are rarely gray or black; they veer toward blue or mauve, crimson or green, as they are colored both by the surfaces on which they fall and by reflection from adjacent objects. Analyze their shapes; like clothes draping a person's body, shadows can be used to describe the forms over which they lie.

Reserving and masking To build up a convincing balance of light and shade, establish the shaded areas of your composition at the outset. This enables you to retain the light and shade pattern that first attracted you to the scene—the shadows will move as the day wears on. Sunlit areas can initially be reserved as white paper, which can be tinted later with a pale transparent wash if the white looks too glaring when the other colors are in place.

Masking fluid can be used to reserve the "negative shapes" between multiple shadows cast by the leaves of trees—the small patches of sunlight. Be specific with your shapes; also mask out highlighted details that stand in front of darker areas so that you can lay the dark washes with confidence.

Glazing An alternative to marking in the shadows at the start is to lay them on with transparent washes over the colors of the landscape. The colors beneath will shine through the transparent wash, creating exciting passages of watercolor. If there is reflected color, use a wet-in-wet wash. While the shadow wash is moist, drop a little color into the side next to the color of the object causing the reflection and let it spread.

Reserving white paper

The bright white paper left unpainted in the sunny landscape creates a strong contrast of light and shade. A light warm glaze of yellow is laid in patches to add to the glow.

1 Draw the dark tree shapes and shadows with an underwash of ocher and cadmium yellow to establish their positions. Paint very wet alizarin and ultramarine over the trees and shadows; then drop cerulean blue into the wet paint.

2 Drop spots of clean water onto the foliage masses to soften them. To make the white paper glow, touch in small washes and brushstrokes of cadmium yellow.

Glazes

Thin glazes of greens, yellows, and pinks are built up in dabs so that the colors overlap and shine through from underneath. The shaded areas are washed over with a glaze of ultramarine blue. A fresh, lively effect of dancing color is created.

1 Build up the foliage with small, dabbed brushmarks in thin, clear washes of color.

2 Lay colors over colors in transparent blobs. Wash in the foreground. As you paint the sky, take the blue into the shadows of the columns.

4 Wash a thin transparent glaze of ultramarine blue over the areas darkened by shadow, painting around the shapes of highlighted leaves and flowers.

3 Paint a glaze of yellow ocher over the blue, shaded side of the columns. Build up the foliage with more dabs of color, one across another.

5 Brush in the foreground shadow, and strengthen the deeper shadows with Prussian blue.

Masking shadows

Use masking fluid applied with a brush to create light and shadow quickly.

1 Lay the masking fluid liberally to reserve the dappled light between the shadows. Mask out areas of foliage you wish to reserve.

2 Paint the background foliage with sap green, Payne's gray, and burnt sienna, and lay a dark wash over the masked area. Let it dry completely.

4 Wash in the flower colors. Soften the hard edges of the masking in the sunlit areas of the foreground by wetting it with a pale lilac wash, which is dabbed off while still wet.

3 Rub off the masking fluid with a finger to reveal the white paper underneath.

Masking and tonal contrast

To protect your brush, coat the hairs with petroleum jelly before dipping it in the masking fluid. Masking out ripples means that movement in the water can be retained under subsequent washes.

1 Paint the masking fluid over the sun, its reflection and the ripples in the water. Flick some frisket onto the paper for splashes of water. Lay a pale background wash.

2 Strengthen the color scheme with strong contrasting color washes. Paint the boys in the boats and their soft reflections.

3 Pick out palm fronds and grasses with strong greens, building up the trees to frame the sunlit area.

4 Darken the foliage with successive layers of descriptive brushstrokes. When thoroughly dry, remove the masking fluid with a finger.

5 Paint a glaze of blue-green over the hard-edged shapes in the dark shallows, left by the masking.

Sunsets

The glorious descent of the sun is a subject that cannot fail to appeal, but it is a difficult one for the artist because it all happens so fast.

The sunset doesn't end when the sun has gone down. The clouds turn redder and the whole sky glows. Rather than trying to capture the very moment when the sun is sinking, spend that time watching the sunset. Make a pencil sketch of the composition of the sky, with color notes about the lightest and darkest clouds, and the color they appear in front of the sun; then make the painting after the sun has gone. The arrangement of the clouds will remain similar.

Reserving paper If you are including the sun, remember that it will be lighter than any other part of the painting, and reserve it from the color wash at the start. Either leave a circle of white paper undampened when you lay your wash, or mask out the sphere with masking fluid. The edges can be softened later with a damp brush if necessary, and can be interrupted with foreground silhouettes and clouds across the sun. These are often tinged by the bright orange light, and this color change in an otherwise dark landscape adds an exciting touch.

Wax resist Reserving the sun with candle wax gives a delightfully soft, slightly blotchy effect rather like the patterns seen by the naked eye if you have looked a little too long at the sun. But remember that you cannot paint over the wax later with any clouds or foreground features.

Variegated wash A variegated horizontal wash is the classic technique for a sky changing from red, through yellow to blue. Prepare all the color solutions separately on your palette before you begin.

To preserve the shape of soft, fluffy clouds, drop them in when the wash is nearly dry. Test at the edge of the paper so you do not ruin the center of the painting by dropping color in when the wash is still too wet. Light clouds can be lifted out with a paper towel while the washes are wet.

Lifting out

Soaking up color with a tissue, or loosening dry washes with a damp bristle brush and then dabbing them with a tissue, enables you to lift light clouds out of a darker wash without having to plan them beforehand.

1 Loosely paint the cloud forms. Drop in darker color, wet-in-wet. Lift out cloud layers with a tissue before the wash dries.

2 Loosen the edges of dried washes with a damp bristle brush before lifting out the color of background clouds with a tissue.

3 Touch in the landscape with indigo, but use India red for the branches that glow orange against the molten sky.

Graduated wash

Mix plenty of burnt sienna in the palette, and lay the wash on dampened paper. Grade the wash so that it is darker in the middle around the horizon, i.e. light, darker, lighter.

1 | Mask out the sun and the reflection. Lay the graduated wash and, while damp, wash in some ultramarine blue to cool the color of the sea. Next, darken the horizon area, while wet, with more burnt sienna.

2 | Touch a little burnt sienna into the dark rocks. Paint the ripples with horizontal dry brushstrokes and, after rubbing off the masking, tint the edges of the reflection and of the sun with yellow.

Variegated wash

Work down the paper with single applications of color and no reworking. Drop in narrow lines of cloud while wet, and lay rocks and foreground when dry. Note that the sea will reflect the color of the sky.

1 | Dampen the paper and lay alternate bands of India red and India yellow, introducing violet. While wet, draw thin horizontal clouds with the tip of the brush.

2 | Create the cloud bank on the horizon with a band of raw sienna and indigo, painted while the wash above is still wet. Do not paint the sea wash until this is dry. Touch in the rocks with a rigger.

3 | Paint the wavelines with a lighter tone than the rocks, and brush in the grasses with dry brushstrokes.

Trees

To paint trees successfully you need to look at the whole shape first. You will be surprised how little detail is then needed.

Seek out the large shapes and masses that characterize the tree or group of trees. Loosely wash in the silhouette, leaving gaps for the sky to peep through, especially near the outer edges and between the trunk and large branches.

You can give a realistic impression of trees using only three tones, so half-close your eyes to find the main areas of light and dark. Use small brushmarks for the suggestion of leaves. To imply the casual elegance of palm trees, paint the fronds by shape rather than individual leaves. Again, three tones should be enough.

Pen and ink To paint branches and twigs you can use a special brush called a rigger; pen and ink is also an effective method and gives a crisp touch to the painting. Try to catch the angles of growth, or the main foliage masses. As branches crisscross, play dark against light to create depth. Take care not to restrict line work to only one area of the picture or it may look disjointed.

Sponging/dry brush Dry paint dabbed onto the foliage masses with a natural sponge is a quick way of suggesting the texture of foliage, and a sponge-applied wet wash will lend life to heavy summer foliage, creating an irregular leafy edge.

The bare tracery of winter trees can be rendered with a dry brush or by the splayed hairs of a wet brush. Look at the networks of branches as a whole and use directional strokes of the brush to indicate growth patterns. Link trunks and branches together with the same color; grays and mauves are convincing colors for winter trees. Dry brush can also be used for the feathered fronds of tropical trees.

Pen and ink

Use a dip pen and waterproof India ink. The definition achieved with the pen is used to draw the composition with gestural lines in order to describe the tree shapes and foliage masses. Thin glazes of color are used to build up the color in the painting.

1 Sketch the painting with the dip pen, lightly at first, and then go over it with a thicker nib. Flick some ink on the foreground bushes.

2 Paint a series of different washes over the dried ink and let them blend, slightly wet in wet. The colors will overlap the drawing and are not confined by it.

3 Wash a glaze of viridian onto the dark side of the trees, again ignoring the edges.

2 Apply a mixture of viridian and yellow with a damp sponge to build up the general shape of the foliage.

3 Add cerulean to yellow-green and pat over the dark and mid-tone areas of the trees. Sketch in branches.

4 Sponge an even darker tone into the dark shadows and draw down the branches while still wet. Darken the trunk with colors that key into the foliage.

5 Last, sponge some yellow ocher on top of the dark foliage to add patches of opacity.

4 Take down the greenness of the trees with a loose wash of rose and Winsor blue, touching it across some of the white areas as you go.

Sponging

Mix a pool of color in the palette and dip a slightly damp natural sponge into the paint. Dab it gently over the tree, repeating the process when the previous layer has dried.

1 Lay a wash of cadmium yellow and pale and cerulean blue.

Dry brush

Applying dry paint to the surface of watercolor paper creates a broken texture as the tooth of the paper picks up the color but the troughs are left untouched. The paint is mixed with just enough water to allow it to leave the brush.

1 Lay a variegated wash of rose, yellow, and cerulean for the background. Sketch in the shapes of the trees with fairly wet paint.

2 Paint the palm fronds with dry brushstrokes, drawing them outward so that the leaves taper.

3 Apply cadmium yellow to the leaves with more dry brushstrokes and then darken them up with slightly wetter, well-defined lines.

4 Lengthen the fronds with long dry brushstrokes, running the dry color down the trunks and into the foreground grasses.

5 The finished picture is alive with color. Movement is suggested by the impression of blurring, created by the dry brushmarks.

Waterfalls

The sound of rushing water, the power, the speed, the spray . . . the subject is daunting, whether majestic Niagaras or small, clear brooks tumbling down into swirling pools.

For the artist the subject is enthralling. The secret of painting moving water is to look for the patterns. Do a couple of line sketches of the flow of the water, keeping your eye on the direction the water is taking around and over rocks. Do not look down at your sketch as you draw or you will lose your way. Watch how the water weaves in and under itself, sometimes almost plaiting itself. Leonardo da Vinci told his students to make studies of the flow of hair to understand the movement of water.

Reserving/masking For a large volume of white water, reserve white paper and indicate the movement with light directional brushstrokes. If the body of water is small, use masking fluid for the strands of running water, the water lines alongside rocks, and so on. When the fluid is dry, pull some of it off by scuffing it with a kneaded eraser to break its solidity. Laying washes over this creates delightful running-water effects.

Wax resist The joy of painting tumbling water is that you don't have to be very accurate. Painting over wax resist will create random splotches of color that look like the surface of frothy, broken water. Drawing the flow of the water with the candle will enhance the direction. Alternatives to candles are white wax crayons or oil pastels.

Spattering/flicking Where spray careens up against a background of dark rocks, spatter or flick some masking fluid in the direction of the spray before you paint, or spatter opaque white as a final stage (see SEAS). Where the background to the spray is itself white water, gently spatter colors you have used for the water over the area.

Further Information
☞
Seas, page 97.

Masking

To avoid hard-edged waterlines created by masking fluid, scuff the dried fluid in the direction of the flow of the fall. Color is then pushed in between the loops and strands created, and repetition of the process creates a mottled effect.

1 Mask over all running water areas. When dry, scuff the masking with a rubber in a downward direction. Wash ocher all over and begin to push color into the scuffed areas.

2 When dry, scuff off more masking to reveal some of the white paper and the blobs of color from the previous wash.

3 Push darker color into the scuffed masked areas and build up the landscape around them in overlaying washes. Darken the rocks.

4 When dry, rub off all the masking and lay a pale blue glaze over the vertical shaded areas of the waterfall.

Wax resist

Applying wax to the paper prevents color from settling. Because the wax sticks unevenly to the tooth of the paper, painting over a waxed area will leave a broken patina. Draw the wax in the direction of the fall. Remember, once you have laid the wax on an area, it will no longer take color.

1 Wet the waterfall area and gently stroke down the flow lines of water with Payne's gray and a size 12 sable brush. When dry, apply candle wax in downward strokes.

2 Wet the paper again and lay more strokes of Payne's gray. When dry, apply candle wax more vigorously. This way, the tonal structure of the falls has been established before the wax prevents more paint from adhering.

3 Paint sepia and light red over the waxing until the contrast is sufficient to show the rushing water. Paint the rocks at the base on slightly damp paper to suggest mist.

4 Scratch out speckles of white paper with a scalpel to "fuzz" the edges of the spray against the dark rocks. Paint the trees and strengthen the rocks.

Spatter/ dry brush/flicking

A combination of dry brush, wet-in-wet, spatter and flicking creates a lively painting of white water. Plan the composition before you begin.

1 | Brush Antwerp blue into a wetted sky. Paint the area of broken water with a dry brush and horizontal brushstrokes.

4 | Hold a toothbrush face down across the dark rocks, and draw the handle of a brush back across the bristles to release a spattering of white paint.

2 | Wet the foreground foam and float pale Payne's gray into it, wet-in-wet. Dry-brush to the edge of the foam.

3 | Paint the background and rocks with strong contrasting darks, overlaying different tones with a small brush to vary the texture.

5 | Flick white paint across the front rocks to create larger splashes of water in the foreground.

Winter

Painting is not just a summer occupation. Bare winter trees, soft light, mists rising from rivers at dawn, and frosts outlining twigs and leaves all make wonderful subjects.

Cool colors capture the essence of a winter landscape. However clear the skies, they are paler and colder in color than summer skies. The hard ground has lost its warmth, and ocher replaces lush greens. Cerulean blue, Payne's gray, Prussian blue, yellow ocher, viridian, alizarin crimson, burnt sienna, and burnt umber are useful colors for your winter palette. Frost and snow are all better off left as the white of the paper, with surrounding colors used to delineate them (see SNOW).

Wet-in-wet To paint mists rising from the ground, dampen the paper above the ground and let your top wash seep into it gently. The soft band of white paper left in between looks just like a winter mist (see MISTS).

A delightful textured effect for a loose wintry sky can be created by painting outside in below-zero temperatures. The thin wash of watercolor actually freezes on the paper, and when it thaws, lovely ice patterns form in the wash. A hot vacuum flask of coffee will help you try out this somewhat unpredictable method.

Dry brush Bare winter trees can be painted with a dry brush, giving the tops of trees a scrubby look. To suggest the barren ground of winter, dry brush over ground washes is effective, and you can use opaque paint to lay a covering of frost.

Scratching/sponging An alternative method for a frosty surface is to scratch paint off with the side of a blade. This creates a rough texture which enhances the impression. Thin white branches and small highlights can also be lifted out with the point of a scalpel.

The straggling foliage clinging to a few branches in winter can be rendered by the irregular texture of dry paint applied with a sponge (see TREES).

Further Information
☞
Mists, page 72.
Snow, page 102.
Trees, page 112.

Scratching off

You will need to use a heavy paper, not less than 140 pound, to be able to scratch boldly into the painting. Use the side of a single-edge razor blade to pull out the color and reveal the white paper underneath. The darker the background, the more effective the scratched marks will be.

1 Paint the silhouette of the tree against a dark background hill. Lay opaque white in curved swirls over the greenish grass in the foreground.

2 When the paint is dry, scratch out the contours of the trunk with bold strokes and use upward and downward strokes to scratch out the color from the brown hill.

3 Continue to scratch out the color, but leave the left-hand side of the trunk and the undersides of the branches as black paint to create an impression of three dimensions in the tree.

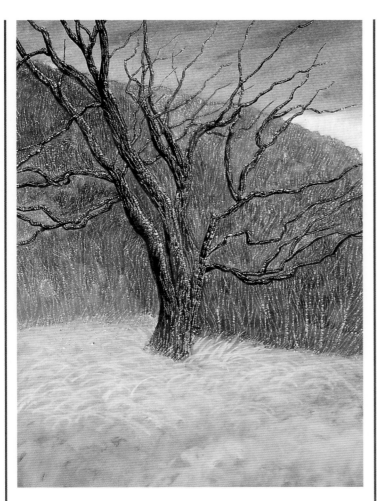

Sponging

Dip a natural sponge in raw umber mixed with Payne's gray. Press it and drag it to suggest the sparse treetop foliage of winter trees.

1 Wash in the sky, reserving white paper for the buildings. Use a touch of lilac near the horizon. Block in the landscape.

2 Drop in darker color for the landscape foliage while the wash is wet. Draw the details of the church and the shadows of branches across the front and roofs.

3 Paint the tree trunks against the skyline and in the village. Dip the sponge into the palette and dab the color onto the trees with a patting, dragging, and slight twisting movement. Softly sponge the trees behind the church and, with a drier, darker color, apply sponging to the dark area to the left.

4 Use longer strokes of the blade above the grass to suggest the frosty stems of bushes. Paint white body color in swirling strokes over the grass.

Themes

The following pages show a gallery of paintings, in which you can see many different pictorial approaches to landscape, as well as a wide variety of subject matter. The paintings are grouped under separate themes, the first dealing with landscape influenced by man. In the later Wilderness section you will see how some artists have interpreted the unfettered landscape of the wild through more unusual compositions and techniques. The second section explores waterscapes – rivers, lakes and streams – while the major subject of seascape, which includes rocky coastlines and beaches, is given a section of its own.

Landscape

The landscape, enhanced, tamed, or marred by human influence, is probably the most accessible outdoor theme for the artist. Different choices of color and technique are explored through seasonal variations.

The success of a painting cannot be measured, nor accounted for, by the study of technique alone. There is a mystery in each painting that is hard to pin down or describe. Atmosphere and mood may be created by the choice of color, tone, and composition, and are strengthened by the techniques employed to apply the watercolor. Most paintings call on more than one technique to create a successful image, but what really makes a painting work has something to do with the artist's personality, the spirit in which it is painted, and the mystery of being able to transfer three dimensions into two dimensions and yet suggest depth. In the following paintings, attention is drawn principally to one main technique in the painting, while others are described in the text; but these descriptions do not adequately explain the reason why a painting works.

The beauty of watercolor is that more can often be said by suggestion than by actual detailed description. The paintings in this section employ a number of techniques to emphasize seasonal color and change, tonal contrast, and wetness. In general, the artists have distilled their subject matter to avoid unnecessary distractions and often contrast very loose painting with crisp-edged features to hold the composition together. As you study the paintings, cover different areas of the picture with your hand and try to decide if one particular area is more essential than another; that is, would the painting still work without this section?

Different papers and brushes also help to create original effects, but more often it is the actual gesture of the brushstroke that contributes to the personality of the painting. Notice how freely, almost carelessly, paint is sometimes applied, and how effective this abandon can be.

PICNIC AT HENLEY
Paul Kenny

The carefree, heady days of summer are epitomized in this lazy summer scene. The picnickers are suggested by brushstrokes of bodycolor painted over a broadly brushed background. The sky wash of cerulean blue has granulated and settled into the tooth of the paper, creating an interesting texture to the sky.

The vitality of the painting rests in the dynamic horizontal brushstrokes of thin bodycolor drawn across the painting with a flat brush. The painting is small and has been painted quickly; rather than having to decide where to reserve white highlights, the artist has restored them with white gouache.

ENVIRONS OF PAMAJERA
No. 105
Alex McKibbin
This lively tropical painting is built up with swift, clean glazes of color. The suggestions of detail are drawn with small, gestural linear brushstrokes on the fronds of the palm trees and on the balcony rails. Dry brushwork is used over the white paper and the glazes, allowing the undercolor to shine through. Notice how the segments of the trunks of the palm trees are shaped with rounded strokes from a flat brush.

PATH TO THE SEA
Charles Penny
Small dabbed brushmarks combine to create this lively, cheerful corner of the Mediterranean. Depth is achieved in this mosaic of color by pushing dark tones in under the light colors of the foliage. The composition appears free and spontaneous, but the opposing diagonals of the flower bank and tree trunks create a V-shaped window through which the distant houses are viewed, making a very strong composition.

ASKRIGG
Bill Taylor
Patches of color are laid with a flat brush to create this painting of a village nestled in the hills. A pleasing combination of translucent earth colors overlay each other in an abstracted pattern of almost geometric brushmarks that hint at, rather than describe, the shapes of the houses, roofs, and trees. This is an excellent example of how little actually needs to be painted to suggest much more.

FIELDS TOWARDS LEWES
Annie Wood
Soft and splotchy, and apparently painted with abandon, this delightful summery painting is, in fact, carefully built up with successive washes of color worked into each other while wet. The strong pencil lines that sketched the composition prior to painting now serve to describe the furrows of the field.

AUTUMN IN GENOA
LaVere Hutchings
The artist has sketched the composition fully before masking the tree trunks and grasses. The color is then built up in thin washes, freely applied, wet-on-dry and occasionally wet-in-wet. After removing the masking, some areas, such as the trees in the middle distance on the right and the foreground grasses lying in the shadow of the tree on the left, are washed over with thin glazes of transparent color.

SEPTEMBER COLOR
James Harvey Taylor
The overall atmosphere conveyed by this autumnal landscape is one of serenity and gentleness. The right-hand trees dissolve wet-in-wet into the background, and autumnal colors merge softly wet-in-wet within the tree shapes themselves. The reserved white paper for the buildings blends crisply but gently beneath the trees. In the foreground, the paint is spattered, splashed, and splotched in a perfectly controlled "frenzy" to create areas of light and shade in the wild meadow grass.

RETREAT
Jann T. Bass

The swathe of white paper reserved for the path, trees, and building makes a vibrant contrast with the rich bronze colors of the landscape, creating a dynamic composition out of simple elements. The slight variations of color within each of the main washed areas are essential to the life of the painting.

TRAVELS WITH A DONKEY
Paul Bartlett

This fearless little sketch is brimming over with humor. The ink is not waterproof, so the artist has avoided smudging the inked areas by leaving white paper around them. These irregular shapes add charm and character to the quality of the painting.

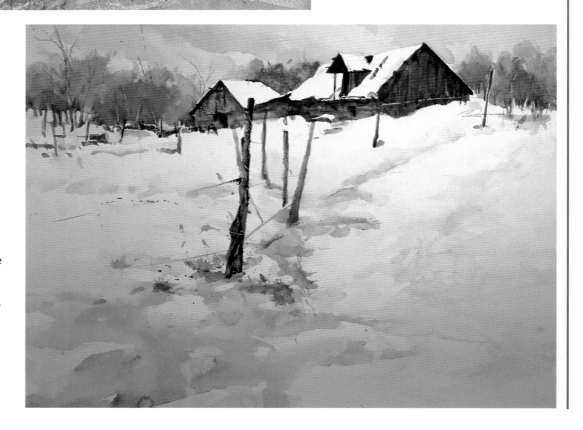

NEAR GOORKHA, NEPAL
Ken Howard
The clear, cold sunlight of a Tibetan temple perched high in the mountains is crisply portrayed with swift brushstrokes in a well-chosen blue. Dry brush is used to describe the stepped pyramid climbing up to the temple. Dabs and linear brushstrokes paint the foliage. The buildings themselves are carefully drawn, and the shadows of the roofs describe their three-dimensional forms. The orange figures reinforce the dramatic scale.

MOUNTAIN WINTER
Jann T. Bass
The high horizon and the large area of reserved white paper create an interesting basic composition. Minimum color is introduced to achieve a contrast of tone that makes a strong statement. The artist then washes loose, sploshy shadow into the foreground area, which highlights the virginal white of the hill.

NINEBANKS
Bill Taylor

The rough cream-colored paper provides a warm overall light to this painting of thawing snow. The composition was sketched with black ink, which is diluted to create the cast shadows. The palette is limited. White is then brushed broadly over the snow-covered areas, picking up the grain of the paper and making blue-grays where it lies over the pure and diluted blacks.

SNOW AT MORSTON
Alan Oliver

The color of the sky influences the wintry mood of this peaceful painting. The artist has tilted the sky wash while wet to create gentle downward runs. The trees are then brushed in wet-in-wet, while the white paper is reserved to add crisp edges to the buildings. The snow-covered fields are separated from the pathway by the thinnest of washes, preserving the luminosity of the bright snow under the gray sky.

DISTANT FARM
Alan Oliver

The freshness of spring is brilliantly carried out in this painting. The individual blooms that make up the carpet of flowers are made by scattering salt crystals carefully over the wet paint so that larger blooms are created in the foreground and smaller ones appear farther back. The light leaves on the tree are dabbed on with gouache bodycolor, making lights against the dark foliage and darks against the sky. (See ROCKS, SALT CRYSTALS)

PATH THROUGH THE WOOD
Alan Oliver

Another lively composition by the same artist imaginatively portrays the pointillist effect of new spring growth through the use of spattered and flicked color. The areas of light and dark are carefully delineated to enable the artist to spatter greens, yellows, and blues in "controlled random" across the painting. The loose, vertical tree trunks and the hard-edged horizontal shadows pull the composition together. (See PATHWAYS, SPATTER)

LANDSCAPE IN BLUES
James Harvey Taylor
This painting has all the *joie de vie* reminiscent of spring, with abundant color beneath a tumultuous sky. If you cover the buildings, the painting is almost abstract. The shapes of reserved white paper are skillfully chosen to describe the rooftops, and the colors are well contrasted.

PUMPKIN MARKET
Naomi Brotherton

This charming night painting shows how bright painted lights can be if they are set against enough tonal contrast. The stream was reserved as white paper and then tinted with colored reflections so that it remains light against the dark ground. The brightness of the light shining out onto the fresh produce is enhanced by the complementary (opposite) colors of blue and orange.

AUTUMN WALK, TRENT PARK
Mark Topham

The enjoyment of this painting is held in the long shadows cast by the low winter sun and the rich overall color. The artist has built up the foliage with layers of washy color, which were laid when the color underneath had dried. Warm browns and mauves are used to create that warmth felt on a sun-kissed winter's day.

BETATAKIN
Judith S. Rein
Here the artist has actually used subtle differences in tone to build up the whole composition in sections, rather like a mosaic. Look carefully at the different tones within each area of blocked tone. Careful drawing is necessary before painting something as complex as this.

POSTS IN SUNSHINE
LaVere Hutchings
This pathway painting is slightly backlit, casting the posts dark against the sky and the top of the grassy bank is light against that same midtone. The highlighted grasses are scratched out of the dark paint on the bank with a sharp blade. (See GRASS, SGRAFFITO)

SUN SHOWER
Becky Haletky
The overall coloring, painted
with a limited palette, creates
the wet, overcast atmosphere
of a faded industrial town. The
streaks of rain laid in diagonal
strokes draw a veil over the
painting, slightly blurring the
image. It takes courage to
draw lines all over a
completed composition.

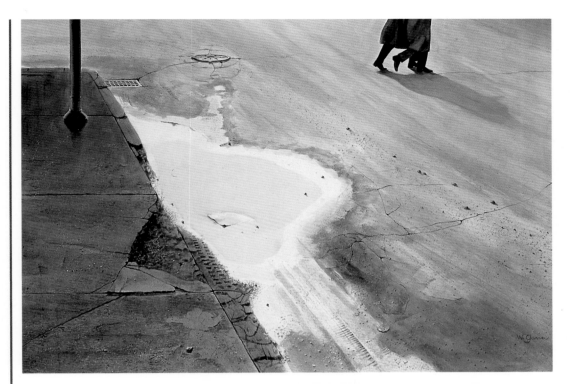

STREET SCENE
Walter Garver
This painting is full of delightful narrative content. Basically, it is the painting of a puddle, but what a marvelous puddle! The figures scurrying away, the shadow cast by the sun coming out after the rain, the glare of gray-white sky mirrored in the water—all these tell a story and combine to make an exciting painting with an unusual composition. Dry brushwork and spatter are used to build up the grainy surface of the road and path. (See PATHWAYS; ROADS)

COULTERVILLE
LaVere Hutchings
This wonderfully executed wet-in-wet technique for a rainy shanty-town painting shows a perfect marriage of technique and subject matter. The softness of all the merged color is controlled by the hard-edged areas of reserved white paper, later tinted with pale glazes. The reflection of the shack is painted into the wet road wash just before it dries so that the vertical side of the building is mirrored softly without the color spreading. (See RAIN)

Waterscapes

The inherent movement of water brings life into a painting, whether the water is fast-moving, languid, or still. The repetition of the landscape in a mirrored or blurred reflection creates a strong and appealing composition.

Several different techniques can be used to achieve similar results. In the paintings that follow, you will see highlights on the water produced by reserving white paper, masking out, lifting out, restoring with bodycolor, or revealing by scratching out. Look carefully at the way in which the artists create the wetness of water, the tonal contrast with the dry land, the movement of the reflected image, and the length of the reflection.

By its very nature, watercolor is well suited to the rendering of water. The wonderful merging of colors wet-in-wet is ideal for the blurred image of an uncertain reflection. The irregular shapes of tiny flecks of white paper left untouched when a wash is laid are perfect for ripples of water catching the light.

The following pages explore paintings of fast-moving water, still water, mirrored reflections, rippled reflections, and blurred reflections. The techniques used for painting the water are many, but paintings are not the sum of their techniques—it is the human touch that gives a painting life.

Looking at these paintings should give you confidence to paint water in different ways. If you are disappointed with your own attempts, see how another artist has tackled water in a similar composition. Few paintings are irredeemable, and always remember that there is usually more than one way to achieve a successful image, even if your first attempt resulted in disaster!

MORNING SPIRE
Paul Kenny

A careful balance of subtle variations in tone creates this tranquil, almost romantic scene. The colors used have a mystical appeal, achieved in part by mixing some of the watercolor with a little opaque paint. The areas of foliage are painted wet-in-wet, greeting the sky with soft, misty edges. The light on the water under the trees has been created by lifting out color from the wash with the strokes of a damp brush just before the wash dries.

Interesting textures on the foliage and water are the result of the pigment settling in the grain of the paper.

The balance of tone is the key to this painting, and you will notice that the artist has used masterly touches of bodycolor to even out the tone on the lower spires of the church. (See MISTS; WINTER, OPAQUE PAINT; BUILDINGS, GRANULATED WASH)

WATERFALL, CUMBRIA
Tom Groom

This fresh rendering of a mountain stream tumbling through a rocky valley is built up with transparent blocks of color applied with a broad flat brush. The whitest whites are reserved white paper where the water finally cascades, frothing, into the stream below. Look at the other whites of the water and you will see that the artist has skillfully taken them slightly back in tone by the use of white bodycolor. This is more apparent in the distant stream, but if you look closely at the last descent, you will see that white paint is used to soften the water's edge against the rocks.

LIBERTY WATERFALL
Shirley McKay

The peaceful background of this river contrasts brilliantly with the exciting foreground. The playful splash of the froth is created by flicking white paint across the dark rocks. As in the previous painting, but with more dramatic contrast, the artist makes the white water shine out brilliantly by darkening the other water around it. (See WATERFALLS, FLICKING)

SNOWSHED SLIDE
Betty Blevins

The detail in this painting is applied over wet-in-wet washes that have fully dried. The artist works carefully from top to bottom, completing each area before moving down the page. Dry brush technique is used to create the broken foamy textures of the fast moving rapids and the wild grass on the bluffs. The shadows over the foreground and the distant bluff are laid with a dark transparent glaze, which is painted over the details when the work is dry. A soft area of white paper is reserved for the steam issuing forth from the funnel of the train. (See RIVERS, MASKING)

TUOLUMNE POOL
Dan Petersen

This painting has almost a fantasy feel to it. The pool of still water through which the rocky bed is revealed changes from blue to orange as it comes toward the front of the picture. The details of the rocks are drawn in first and, when it is dry, the colorful glaze is washed over the top. The use of perspective is quite dramatic, bringing the painting from far away directly to the viewer's feet.

FISHIN' UPSTREAM
Betty Carr

Vibrant brushwork creates a lively watercolor full of movement. The undercolor is applied wet-in-wet, and fast brushstrokes are laid on top to describe the trees and river edge. The movement of the figure and the flight path of the fishing line scratched out from the painted surface create a focus that takes the eye back and forth across the painting. The tiny bands of light water left trailing from the fisherman's boots are essential to suggest the movement in this painting.

AROUND THE BEND
Sue Kemp

In this watercolor, distance is skillfully achieved by the perspective of the river and the change to a very light tone at the bend in the flow. Beyond, the glazes of color are laid simply over dried washes, while the smooth flow of the water is described with a wet-in-wet wash.

LOW TIDE, DISTANT RAIN
Robert Tilling R.I.

The artist has worked this painting very wet indeed, using large brushes absolutely loaded with paint. After laying the paint in sweeping brushmarks, he then tilts the board. Wonderful granulated patterns are created as the paint settles.

AVON RIVER NEAR CHRISTCHURCH
Donald Pass

To achieve the appearance of the sparse, dry winter foliage bordering the glassy river, the artist has used a combination of dry brush and sponging. Small highlights are then scratched out with a blade. The techniques employed are well suited to the subject matter; a cool breath of winter is created in the foreground, and a certain warmth in the middle distance and background is created from burnt sienna and umber washes. The dark tones brushed in for the reflections of the river banks add to the sense of still water created by the mirrored reflections of the trees.

ISLANDS OFF WEST COAST OF SCOTLAND
Kay Ohsten

The beauty of watercolor as a medium is that it can quickly record a scene, as this simple silhouette of rocks and sea shows. The sparkles in the foreground are left in the white paper by brushing the wash lightly across the tooth of the paper to create a shimmering sea. (See SEAS, VARIEGATED WASH)

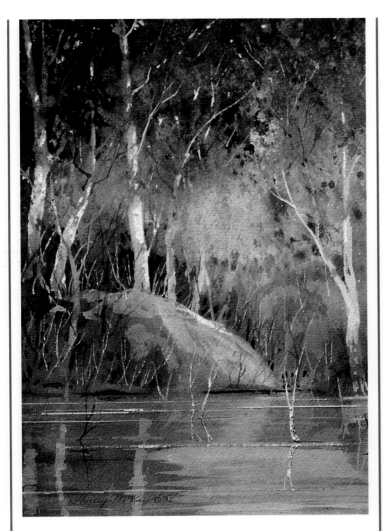

HIDDEN POND
Shirley McKay
A sense of privacy is felt as the viewer enters this painting of a secret glade. The still water is portrayed by gentle horizontal strokes, and the light trunks of the trees have been masked out and then glazed over. The charming background colors merge together wet-in-wet.

AUTUMN REFLECTIONS
Mark Topham
The puddle reflects the warm, pale gray of the winter sky above the trees. No other part of the painting is as light as this area. The viewer is convinced of the puddle's wetness by the reflection of the trees. Note the part of the tree and fence that is mirrored in the puddle.

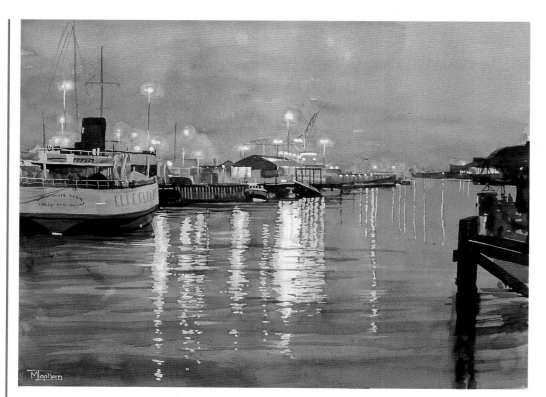

EVENING LIGHT, NEW HAVEN HARBOUR
Mark Topham
In this atmospheric night painting, the artist has used masking fluid to reserve the lights on the dock and the long, rippled reflections in the dark water. The sky and water have been generously washed in above and below the quay. The halos of light are lifted out from the sky and tinted with yellow. Once the frisket is removed, some small dark ripples are painted over the reflections to break the columns of light. (See NIGHT, MASKING)

THIS IS THE PLACE
Betty Carr
Using bold brushstrokes over dried washes, this painting relies on strong contrasts of tone to build a vibrant rippled-water effect. The reflections of the rocks themselves are much lighter than the strong foreground, making a vital shift in perspective from the front of the painting to the middle distance.

ENVIRONS OF PAMAJERA
Alex McKibbin
At close hand, the application of brushstrokes and glazes appears rather random, until you pull back from the painting and see how brilliantly the perspective falls into place. The river leads gracefully away between the banks, with its surface patterned by light and shadows cast from the umbrella of overhead trees. The long, dry brushstrokes are often used directionally to describe the verticality of tree trunks or the flatness of water.

EVENING GARDEN
Rebecca Patman
The fragmented lights on the rippled water in this charming garden painting are created by reserving white paper. The water is painted wet-in-wet, leaving flecks of white paper as the color is laid and successfully mirroring the colors of the background it reflects. More ripples are painted across the surface of the water when the wash is dry.

COTERIE
Jann T. Bass
Although the water in this landscape is frozen, ice still reflects something of the features above it. The tree trunks are brushed down into the ice with fairly pale, dry strokes. The geese stepping onto and across the ice tell the viewer that the surface is solid, while the subtle reflections and color show the surface as ice.

RESERVOIR LIGHT
Robert Tilling R.I.
Working with large brushes and abundant paint, the artist uses sweeping brushstrokes to lay the washes. He then tilts the board to let the paint run into drifting reflections, allowing the effect more importance than an accurate reflection would. The color is then scraped back to create two bands of light across the water.

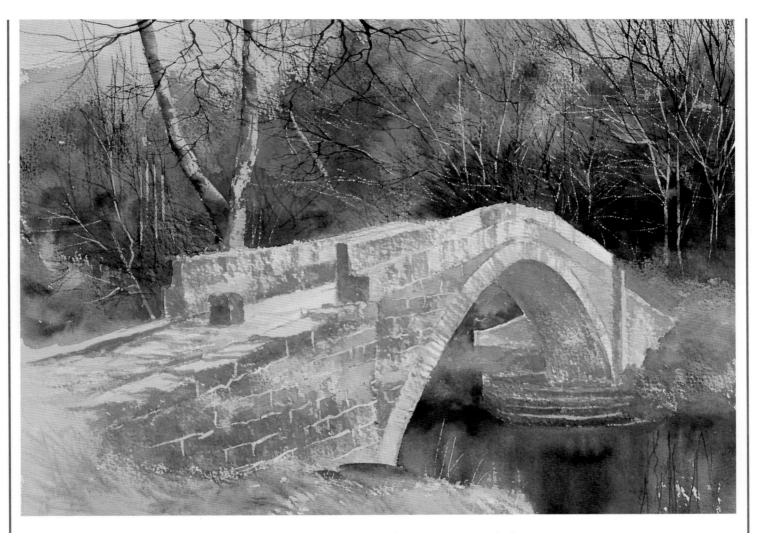

BRIDGE
R. H. Pearson

This cheery painting of a bridge in winter is painted using many different techniques. The background and water are washed wet-in-wet. The color of the foreground is applied mainly with dry brushwork. The mortar of the brickwork and the narrow tree trunks have been masked out, then tinted. The skeleton branches of the winter trees are scratched out with a blade, while the dark branches are painted with a long-tipped rigger. Darks are placed against lights throughout the painting to give a strong tonal composition. (See BRIDGES)

Wilderness

The wild, untrammeled regions of our planet allow the artist to find expression for grandeur, vastness, and solitude. These qualities present wonderful opportunities to play with color and technique in a less restrained way.

Jungle, woodland, mountains, valleys, canyons, rock formations, moorland, veld, and tree lines are among the subjects represented in this section. By the nature of the subject matter, some of the paintings display strong color, vibrant contrasts, dramatic compositions, and a freedom of paint. Others pick out intimate corners of the wild landscape or bathe the subject in an all-pervasive tranquility.

To be alone in nature that is untouched by human hand is uplifting and humbling. Sometimes it is overwhelming. The artist must choose the elements of the view that he or she most wants to paint, and leave out the rest. Once the choice of composition is established, you can be daring or subdued with your color, wild or sensitive with your brushstroke.

Do not feel obliged to represent your subject accurately. Moving a rock to the right or left to help the composition is part of creating a painting. If you are afraid of your own ability, position yourself in a place where the composition laid out before you is pleasing to the eye, or interesting in design, and then you can simply "copy" nature! Color can also be exaggerated to enhance the mood you are trying to express. Always remember that the painting must stand alone, away from the landscape, with nothing to compare it to. Even if you are painting a well-known feature, you need not feel restricted; your interpretation of the landscape is special to you, and that is what others appreciate when they view the painting.

BANKS OF THE ORINOCO
Hazel Soan

The artist has sought to create some order out of the luxuriant chaos of this South American jungle. The fronds of the palms and the twists of the lianas are masked out from the equatorial profusion so that wet-in-wet washes can be freely applied across the foliage and then diverse colors dropped into the washes while they are wet.

The frisket is then removed and glazed with more color in places, while some areas are kept as virgin white paper. White bodycolor is used to establish the ripples on the water.

EXPRESSIONS
Bernice Alpert Winick
This exciting painting draws on strong vibrant color applied wet-in-wet. The pigment is mixed in strong solutions and boldly painted with sloshes of color. Control is exercised in the areas of light and dark tone, but the watercolor is allowed to make its own wonderful combinations of color between areas of stillness and areas of dynamism.

ENVIRONS OF PAMAJERA
Alex McKibbin
The composition is built up with vivacious directional glazes using a flat brush and wet and dry pigment. Interesting color combinations emerge from the overlays of color. The irregular-shaped "bands" of white paper, reserved as lights between the strokes, narrow as they recede, strengthening the perspective of the avenue between the trees.

ARMONIOSO
Bernice Alpert Winick
A dynamic and intriguing painting is created by the strong diagonal composition and the energetic runs of paint. The background is painted wet-in-wet. The artist has tilted the paper in all directions to encourage the paint runs to become the flexible limbs of trees and the searching lines of roots. Bodycolor is mixed with the watercolor to create opaque glazes.

LIGHT AND SHADOW
Jerry Wray
The engaging color of this delightful tangle of woodland scenery is built on the play of opposites. Mauve and yellow are complementary colors, as are red and green. The contrast of opposite colors creates vibrancy. The artist lays a film of clear plastic over the wet paint and then works into the patterns produced to give form to the landscape.

MOUNT OLYMPUS
Shirley McKay
A sky of looming rain clouds
billows over the snow-clad
mountains. The clouds are
painted wet-in-wet with dark,
thundery color dropped into
the damp white areas. The
fluidity and shape of the
clouds gives them their
movement, and the dark
purplish color offsets the white
mountain top. White bodycolor
is used undiluted or with
pigment to make opaque
glazes on the wooded ridges.
(See CLOUDS; WET-IN-WET)

MOUNT OLYMPUS OF THE
WASATCH
Willamarie Huelskamp
In this painting, the artist does
not use overall washes to
build up her mountain;
instead, each area of tone and
color is painted separately. The
color laid is the final one. The
three-dimensional form of the
ridges and valleys is
accentuated by the sideways
light, and achieved by using
strong, dark tones in the
crevices contrasted with the
light on the ridges. (See
MOUNTAINS; HILLS)

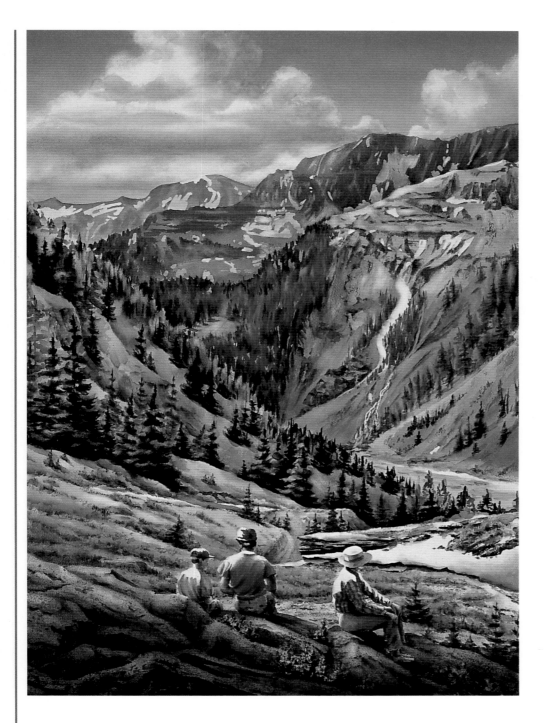

YANKEE BOY BASIN
Betty Blevins

This fairly complex subject is built up in an orderly fashion, successfully projecting the smallness of the figures in this grand panorama. The artist masks out the snow and figures first, then completes each area, working down the page, before proceeding with the next. A wet-in-wet underwash is laid and allowed to dry. The details are painted over the wash. When the masking is removed from the snow areas, these spaces are glazed with pale versions of their respective mountain colors to help them recede into the distance. The figures are painted last, with white paper left for the sun's highlights.

BRYCE CANYON, WINTER SHADOWS
Willamarie Huelskamp

Before painting, the artist carefully delineates the different areas of tone and color. Areas of the same color are then painted with strong, vibrant washes. Almost no overpainting occurs, except the delightful overlap of edge lines where two colors meet. Careful attention is paid to the different tones within an area. The result is a strong painting that comes together magnificently from a short distance away.

MOONSPUN
Mary Ann Brandt

This nocturnal sketch is painted with the fingers on a smooth surface so that the paint can be manipulated easily. As the paint is "smeared" into the shapes of the mountains and valleys, the residue of the pigment stains the paper slightly, creating enjoyable textures and a painting full of gaiety and light.

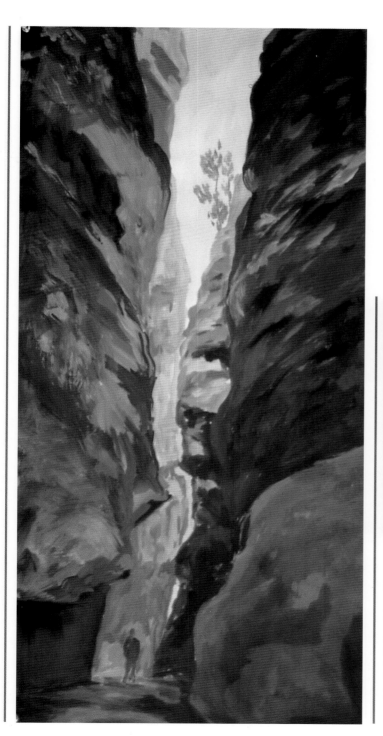

BRYCE CANYON
Angie Nagle Miller

The steep walls of the canyon make an exciting composition, with the dramatic scale indicated by the figure silhouette at the base. Using casein watercolor and bristle brushes, the artist works the paint into wet washes, blending the color on the paper. Some dry brushwork is also used. The opaque paint gives a tremendous solidity to the rocky ravine.

PACIFIC ISLAND
Jerry Wray

This landscape is part of a series called "Places Remembered." Rather than painting directly from the scene, the artist uses an unusual technique to recreate the island wonderland from patterns on the paper. First he pours diluted watercolor on damp paper, and then he loosely lays a covering of clear plastic film, letting it crumple into the wet paint. When dry, he removes the plastic and seeks out the landscape from the textured print on the paper, creating a landscape by using his imagination.

CANYON SENTINEL
Shirley McKay
Strong color and a simple, direct approach are used to create an image of grandeur. The sunlight passing between the clouds touches the side of the flat-topped mountain in the middle of the painting, making an enjoyable change of tone. The artist has cleverly used running drips of color to form a pattern of crevices in the peaked mountain.

GENESIS
Hazel Soan
To establish this glacial tumble of granite rocks in three-dimensional space, the artist has concentrated first on building up the forms tonally. Note that the background rocks are all slightly paler to help them recede. While the strong, dark colors are still wet, color is dropped into the wet washes and allowed to spread. The grainy textures of the granite boulders are created by liberally sponging paint in fairly strong colors over the surfaces. (See ROCKS)

EARTH'S RAINBOW
Willamarie Huelskamp

This dynamic painting is a wonderful example of the vibrant strength of complementary colors on the picture surface, and of the nature of blue to recede and orange/red to come forward. The contrast of the blue with the orange makes each color more intense. The artist does not overlap colors to form new colors, as in traditional watercolor techniques. Instead, she draws the shapes and areas of different color, and then literally fills them in with a few chosen colors mixed on the palette. The dark lines formed where the colors overlap cause the lighter colors to glow more brightly.

SLEET ON THE MOOR
Bart O'Farrell

With the shower of sleet extending its icy fingers across the empty moor, the bleakness of this scene is perfectly set. The flurries of sleet are created by using salt crystals to soak up the pigment from the black winter clouds, and they are spread in a wonderful curving swathe. Dry brush is used for the scrubby moorland grass. (See ROCKS, SALT CRYSTALS; GRASS, DRY BRUSH)

SPRING SEA
Robert Tilling R.I.

To achieve this broad, open landscape, the artist lays very wet paint with a large brush. The hills are painted in just before the sky wash dries to create the broken edge, which is reminiscent of the leafy tops of trees. This painting shows how much can be achieved with one color and several tones.

THE TURN OF THE
SEASONS
Hazel Soan
The writhing, twisting tree
forms, though dead, give life
to this painting of an empty
water hole in the African bush.
White paper has been reserved
for delicate highlights on the
tree trunks and rocks. Small
areas of the trunks have been
painted wet-in-wet.

HEAT AND DUST
Hazel Soan
The overall golden color of the African landscape is rendered with an underwash of yellow ocher laid on dampened paper, leaving a section untouched in the middle for the rising dust. The wildebeest are painted with successively darkening tones over the pale dusty area. The patina of scrubby foliage is described with dabs from a natural sponge patted on while the wash is still damp. To create the tufts of veld grass, color is dropped into the wet foreground wash and allowed to bloom. (See DESERTS)

YELLOWSTONE FIRE XXXIV
Donald Holden
The drama and brightness of this forest fire is enhanced by darkening the tree forms in front of the blaze. The paint is applied wet-in-wet, mixing the colors on the paper. Subtle variations of tone create the layers of trees.

EARLY MORNING LIGHT
Jerry Wray
This bright vivacious painting suggests an almost magical landscape. The color is brighter, due to the use of complementary opposites— that is, blues next to oranges —and the spreading of the colors wet into wet.

MUELLER PARK
Shirley McKay
The lively use of brushmarks and spatter adds verve to the foreground of this autumnal landscape. A wonderful sense of perspective is created by the gradually diminishing hill forms, taking the eye back to the mountains and beyond to the clouds. The complementary contrast of mauve against yellow throws the golden trees forward to the front of the picture plane.

Seascapes

The sea is always an evocative subject, offering the artist restless moods and serene vistas. The option of distant horizons, sparkling seas, or broad beaches creates enjoyable perspectives and interesting compositions.

The diverse techniques available to the watercolorist can be explored by painting imaginative seascapes. Wax resist, masking, or reserving the white paper are excellent techniques for retaining the whiteness of the paper for foam and broken waves. Alternatively, these whites can be restored by scratching out and adding bodycolor when the painting is complete.

The vast skies that often accompany seascapes are a wonderland for wet-in-wet techniques, variegated washes, backruns, or for tilting the paper to create drifts of color. The animated surface of the sea is a marvelous area to lay on washes that allow the tooth of the paper to break up the wash and create the sparkle of light on water.

As the overall colors are harmonious, a sea and sky composition makes a good subject for practicing techniques that rely on tone rather than color to create interest. Try using just one color in many different tones, or experiment with a very limited palette of two, or at most three, colors.

The broad expanse of beaches, warm and inviting in the foreground, are fun areas in which to practice glazes for shadows, or textural effects such as flicking and spattering. Watercolor is always well suited to a wet subject matter, and the sea is probably the most exciting subject. Do not be afraid to mix plenty of color and apply the paint liberally.

DURDLE DOOR
Leslie Worth

A wonderful hazy apparition of light and shadow is presented in this painting of a natural rock archway formed out of the cliff face. The airy quality of the painting plays games with the solid substance of the rock and the ethereal nature of shadows. The composition of backlight and forward shadows creates an exciting contrast of tone across the picture surface, the mauve shadows commanding a gentle presence across the pale sunlit water.

BRANCASTER, NORFOLK
Kay Ohsten
With relatively few colors and
quick, deft brushstrokes, the
artist has filled this sunset
sketch with life. The color of
the still water is washed in at
the outset, with white paper
reserved to highlight the
mirror-effect of the glassy lake.

AUTUMN MIST
Robert Tilling R.I.
Here is a subject painted with very wet washes and copious quantities of paint. The soft edge of the base of the rocks creates the impression of rising mist, while the top of the silhouette is painted against dry color for a hard edge. Note the warm brown color pushed into the dark clouds.

SANIBEL STORM
Benjamin Eisenstat
The artist has worked quickly while the storm is blowing to capture the wind and rain battering the west coast of Florida. Drama is created with fast brushstrokes and dry brushed trees, with the tree fronds teased out by the strong winds. A touch of bodycolor lightens the puddle on the ground, reflecting the light from the sky above. (See TREES, DRY BRUSH)

A DUSTING OF DUSK
Hazel Soan

The two paintings on this page depict the same harbor in Guernsey in the Channel Islands. Each is built up with one color in successively darkening tones to create a different atmosphere at a different time of day. The highlights are reserved white paper, for which fairly careful drawing was necessary beforehand. An underwash of yellow ocher was laid over everything that was not to remain white. When dry, it was followed with ever-darkening washes of yellow ocher mixed with a touch of alizarin crimson and ultramarine blue.

MELLOW BLUENESS
Hazel Soan

The white highlights were reserved from a pale blue wash. The sea was painted fairly dry to catch the tooth of the paper and create the sparkle of light on rippled water. The layers of blue were gradually built up using wet washes over dry. It is worth comparing the overall warmth of the ocher in *A Dusting of Dusk*, above, with the coolness of this painting to see how color can create atmosphere and mood.

MANEMISMA HARBOR, MARTHA'S VINEYARD
Trevor Chamberlain R.O.I. R.S.M.A.
Swift, deft brushstrokes come together to make a lively harbor scene. Dry brushwork is used to hint at the rigging, while glazes of neutral darks are laid for the shadows. The figure moving between the house and the boat creates an interesting focal point for the narrative of the painting.

EARLY LIGHT, NEWHAVEN HARBOUR
Mark Topham
In this harbor scene, the glassy water shines white against the strong darks of the mooring posts. The reflections in the dark ripples are applied wet-in-wet and wet-on-dry, suggesting the ever-changing momentum of the water. Although there is color in this painting, the strength of the work relies on the strong tonal play of lights and darks running through the perspective.

CRYSTAL PIER, WRIGHTSVILLE BEACH, N.C.
Neil Watson

Here the dynamic perspective is almost drawn with the paint rather than painted. The drag lines of the little boats across the sand follow the strong perspective lines of the pier. The complicated detail of the pier is balanced by the large sandy area so that the eye begins in the foreground and wanders beside the pier.

NORFOLK COAST
Alan Oliver

This deceptively simple painting explores the wet, washy qualities of watercolor. Drifts of color are formed by tilting the paper while the washes are wet. Swift ink lines demarcate the main compositional directions and pull the painting together.

HAZY GLINT
Jann T. Bass
The bright highlights in this attractive painting are created both by reserving white paper and by scratching off. Look at the wavelets breaking on the edge of the shore to see how effectively the scratched-off highlights enhance the broken foam. A little spattering of color enlivens the beach in the foreground.

EARLY MORNING, DELL QUAY (Detail)
Tom Groom
The little boats in this painting have a lot of character. Very few details are needed, but accurate drawing and a descriptive use of tone are of the utmost importance. The painting is built up with fairly dry washes. The mooring lines are drawn with light opaque paint, making their journeys across the picture plane an exciting element of the composition.

NORTH POINT, BARBADOS
D. Warren
The successful use of wax resist, masking, and scratching out combine to create the turmoil of a wild sea meeting a rocky point. Both the rocks and the waves are full of lively textures, drawing the eye into an exciting pattern on the picture plane itself and in the illusion of reality. (See WATERFALLS; SEAS; RIVERS)

WINTER LIGHT, HIGH TIDE
Robert Tilling R.I.
This evocative image of the rocky seashore is painted with an interesting, well-chosen palette. The artist lays the paint in abundant, very wet washes. When they are dry, he scrapes back the color to create the light, watery horizon which glistens under the dark brooding rocks.

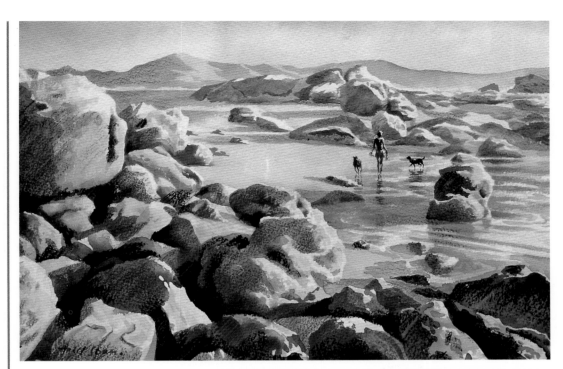

EXPLORING THE EDGE
Hazel Soan
The lights and shadows in this painting are established at the outset with washes of Prussian blue. Care is taken to suggest that the boulders have three dimensions. Ochers and siennas are then washed into the light and dark areas to bring in warmth. The dark tones are overlaid with pencil crayon to strengthen the tones and create textures as the crayon picks out the tooth of the paper (300-pound Not). The silhouette of the woman walking her dogs gives scale to the scene.

LLEYN COASTLINE
Tom Groom
Here again, the tooth of the paper is used to create texture in the painting, but this time by laying dry washes over the rocks and sea so that the pigment brushes only across the top of the grain. The delightful little houses are sketched with the brush and then blocked in with a flat brush.

MIRAGE
Jann T. Bass
A painting need not fill the entire area of the picture plane, as this charming painting of a palm-fringed beach so ably demonstrates. The washes are laid fairly wet and quite diluted, and white bodycolor is used to create highlights. The perspective and movement of the figures as they frolic on the beach are well drawn with one-touch brushstrokes. (See FIGURES)

CLIFFS, HUNSTANTON
Andrew Pitt
One-touch brushstrokes are also used in this painting for the silhouettes of figures dotted along the beach. The wetness of the beach at low tide is painted with a lovely blue of almost the same tone as the sand, reflecting the color of the sky above. This wetness is enhanced with reflections beneath the little rocks and stones.

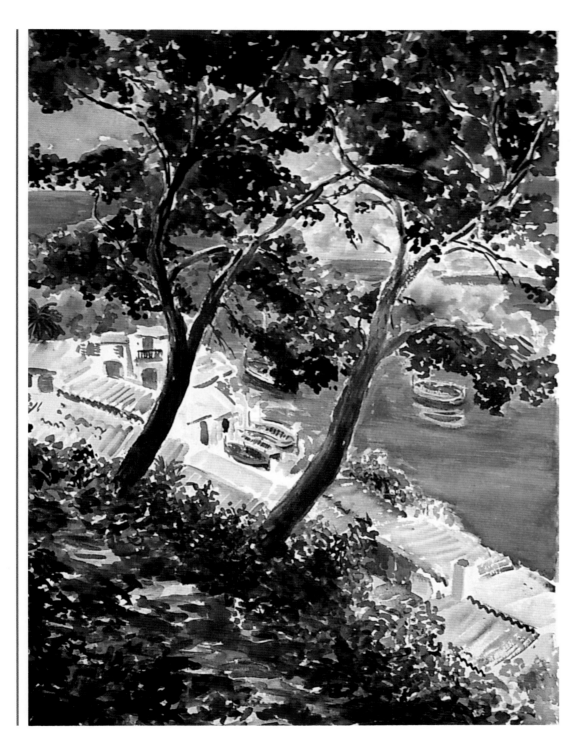

PATH TO THE SEA II
Charles Penny
Cheerful color and almost playful brushmarks combine to create a painting full of warmth and sunshine. The dark foreground contrasts with the light houses below the trees and brings the pathway forward to the viewer. The artist successfully translates an unusual angle of view onto the picture plane, creating a painting full of interest.

Index

Page numbers in *italics* refer to illustrations

Credits

Quarto would like to thank all the artists who kindly allowed us to publish their work in this book.

We would also like to thank all the artists who did painting demonstrations:
Hazel Soan, Rima Bray, Jean Canter, Pip Carpenter, Jane Hughes, Deborah Manifold, Mark Topham, Annie Wood.